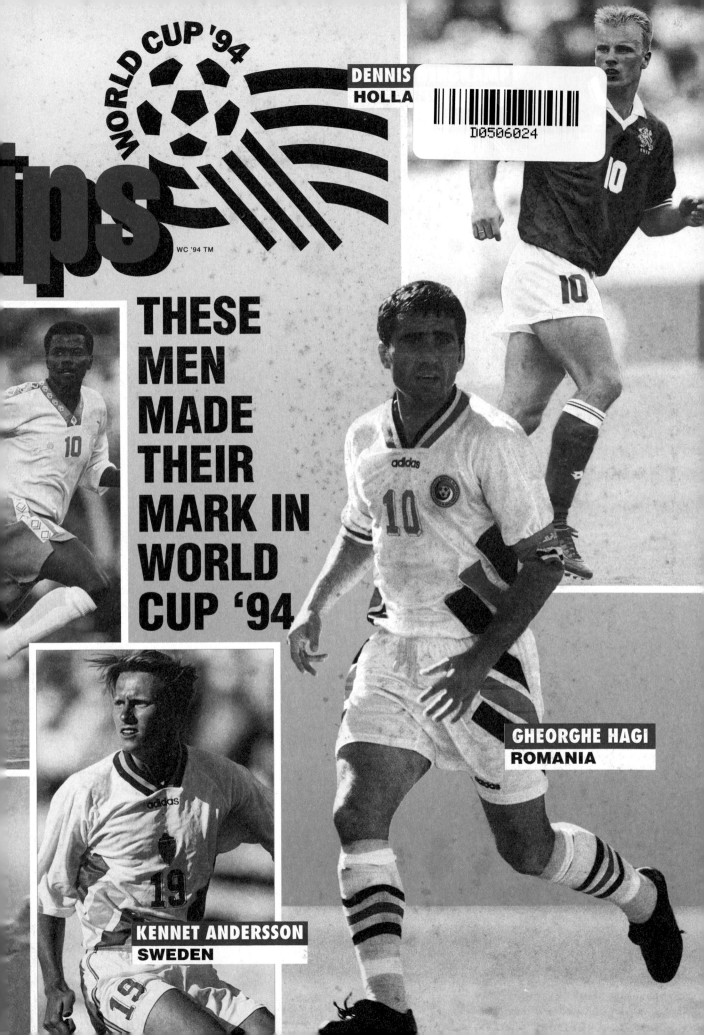

WORLD CUP '94

WC '94 TM

tips

DENNIS
HOLLA

THESE MEN MADE THEIR MARK IN WORLD CUP '94

GHEORGHE HAGI
ROMANIA

KENNET ANDERSSON
SWEDEN

The Topical Times football book 1995

conte

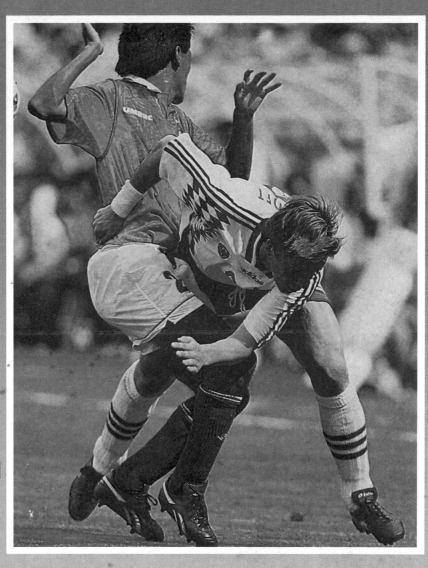

nts

young

● Jason McAteer.

JACK CHARLTON will attempt to lead the Republic of Ireland on a glory trail in the 1996 European Championships and then bid farewell to the international arena.

It's a similar scenario for many of the Irish 'old guard' who have served Charlton and Ireland well over the past few seasons in World Cups and European Championships.

But while such players as Paul McGrath, Ray Houghton, Andy Townsend and John Aldridge may not be around for the next World Cup campaign, the future looks assured for Ireland.

Despite the disappointment at failing to progress beyond the last 16 in America, Charlton will take heart from the performances of his 'young guns'.

And, in particular, centre-half Phil Babb, full-back Gary Kelly and midfielder Jason McAteer returned from the World Cup with their reputations enhanced.

That's a huge source of relief for the Irish FA, who were wary of the threat that once the present crop of talented players had gone through the system, there may not be sufficient resources to replace them.

Phil Babb was the biggest success story of the finals for Ireland. The Coventry City skipper went to America not even certain of his place in the side.

But impressive performances in the warm-up matches persuaded Charlton to give Babb the nod ahead of experienced campaigners such as Kevin Moran and Alan Kernaghan.

Babb's partnership with Paul McGrath in the heart of the Ireland defence was rock solid. Ireland conceded only four goals in their four matches, but a lack of goals at the other end meant that the defensive heroics weren't

● Getting stuck in — Phil Babb clears from Norway's Ovuind Leonhardsen.

guns

enough.

It's Babb's greater maturity which has been a significant factor in his sudden rise to the international ranks.

Last season he was given the Coventry City captaincy, and that responsibility has had a beneficial effect on his game.

"Being given the captaincy has steadied me down, particularly my off-field antics," says the 23-year-old. "Though I'm no rebel-rouser, I used to be a bit unreliable.

"My main problem concerned punctuality. I love my bed and some mornings didn't get up early enough for work.

"That doesn't help much if you are trying to set an example. Being made captain means that I've had to waken my ideas up . . .

"That may be the one reason why I was given the captaincy. Manager Phil Neal knew it was a quick way to sort me out. I have responsibilities and don't intend to let anyone down.

"I have calmed down and adopted a more professional approach. I concentrate fully on the game these days."

Gary Kelly's rise to prominence last term was even more staggering. At the beginning of last season the 20-year-old was on the Leeds sidelines hoping for a few matches in the first team. By its end he was destined to be a World Cup star.

"I was just hoping to make the breakthrough at Leeds," he recalls. "My top ambition at the start of last season was to be in the side by May. Making Ireland's World Cup side exceeded every dream I ever had."

Kelly is the youngest of seven boys — and he also has six sisters! His family ties created problems in his early days at Leeds.

"Being used to such a big family, I was very homesick when I first arrived at Leeds. That's still true to a lesser extent.

"But manager Howard Wilkinson has been great in letting me go home as often as possible. In fact,

everybody at Leeds has been great in helping me to settle."

Jason McAteer can thank an impressive FA Cup run for his inclusion in Ireland's World Cup squad last summer.

Until then the Bolton Wanderers player had been just another promising First Division newcomer learning his trade.

But starring roles in victories over Everton, Arsenal and Aston Villa convinced Jack Charlton that he was ready to make the step up to international football — despite never playing in the top league.

But, as the Birkenhead-born star explains, his performances also alerted England, who joined in an international tug-of-war for his services.

"Jimmy Armfield, the FA liaison man, phoned me on the Friday to say I was in Terry Venables' plans and asked if I would be interested in selection for the England B set-up.

"I was overcome by England's interest and said yes to most of Jimmy's questions. But I didn't make a full commitment.

"On the following Monday I saw Jack Charlton. He asked if I wanted to be in his senior squad for the upcoming match against Russia at Landsowne Road in March.

"Some people have said that I chose the Republic only because I had a better chance of being picked. That's nonsense.

"I believe the Republic are just as strong in their midfield department as England."

With Babb, Kelly and McAteer, now set to be mainstays in the Ireland set-up for the next decade, Jack Charlton knows that his adopted country's football future on the international stage is in safe hands.

● Gary Kelly

ROBERTO BAGGIO

ITALY

ROMARIO   **BRAZIL**

Ahmed Bahja, Morocco.

If Roger Miller and Cameroon taught us anything during Italia '90, it was the fact that the rest of the footballing world was catching up with Europe and South America quicker than we ever imagined.

Cameroon's World Cup victories over Argentina, Colombia and Romania, as well as an epic battle with England, earned Africa an extra place in last year's USA '94 World Cup, and before the tournament, much was expected of the African contingent of Nigeria, Morocco, and Cameroon.

Nigeria, the African champions, were the standard bearers for the continent and their success in finishing top of their group justified the extra place allocated to Africa. Some of their players, like Daniel Amokachi and Augustine Okocha, became household names because of their exploits.

Everybody will remember how desperately unlucky the Nigerians were in their second round game against Italy. They seemed to be cruising to victory over the lacklustre Italians, yet defensive naivety allowed Roberto Baggio to equalise in the dying seconds, and Italy went on to win the game.

Nigeria went home with their heads held high, but they showed the world that Cameroon's success in Italy wasn't a flash-in-the-pan.

Unlike Nigeria, Cameroon and Morocco both went home without a victory, but their performances offered enough evidence to show that African football can produce a World Cup winner in the near future.

Cameroon, wracked by in-fighting and Presidential interference, will be remembered for their 6-1 defeat by Russia, but they did force a draw with semi-finalists Sweden and gave Brazil a tough time until defender Song was dismissed for a professional foul.

Morocco lost every game, but each by the narrowest of margins. They gave Holland and Belgium a very rough ride in Orlando, and proved Northern Africa can compete just as well as Central Africa.

The prospects are healthy in Africa. Non-qualifiers such a Ghana, Ivory Coast and Zimbabwe all possess players, like Nii Lamptey and Peter Ndlovu, who perform throughout Europe. When France '98 comes around there will be four African nations, so their chances of winning the World Cup will increase again.

Africa may have enhanced its growing reputation in the USA, but it was another area of the world which stole the headlines during the com-

out of the shadows

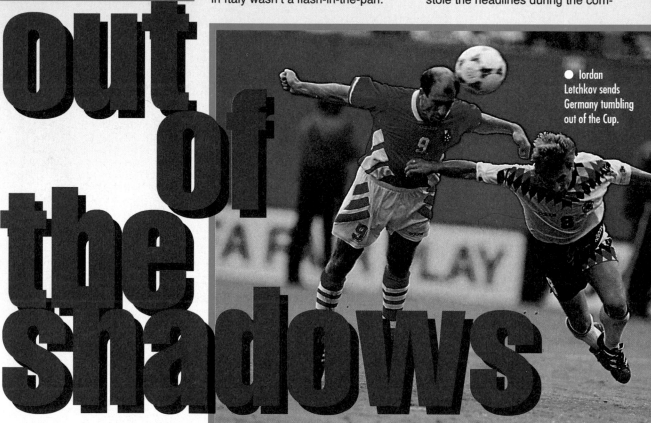

● Iordan Letchkov sends Germany tumbling out of the Cup.

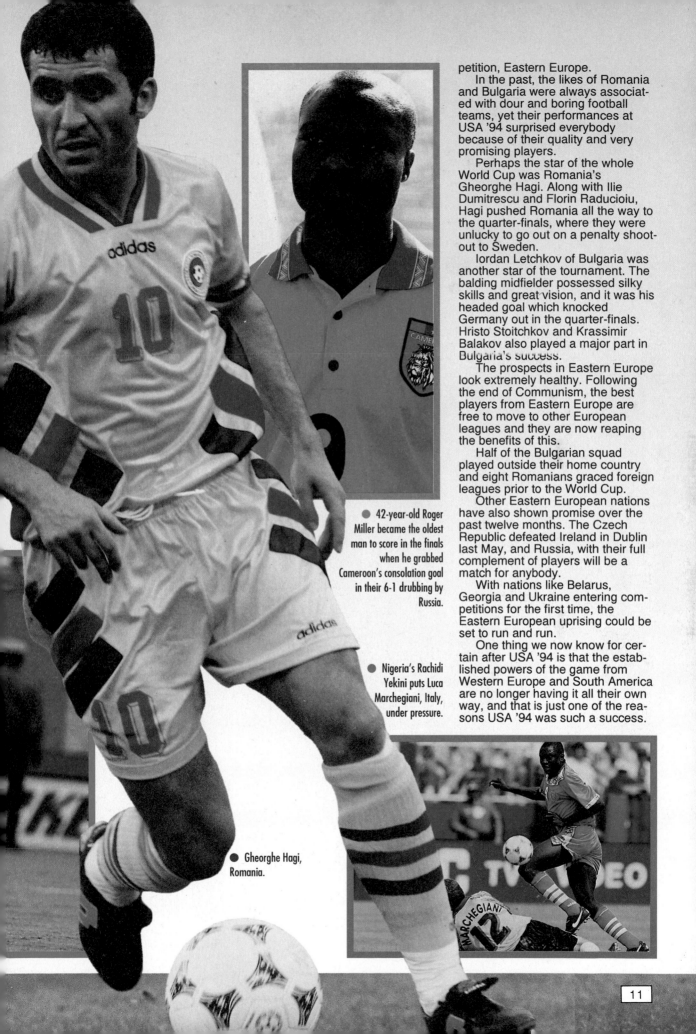

petition, Eastern Europe.

In the past, the likes of Romania and Bulgaria were always associated with dour and boring football teams, yet their performances at USA '94 surprised everybody because of their quality and very promising players.

Perhaps the star of the whole World Cup was Romania's Gheorghe Hagi. Along with Ilie Dumitrescu and Florin Raducioiu, Hagi pushed Romania all the way to the quarter-finals, where they were unlucky to go out on a penalty shoot-out to Sweden.

Iordan Letchkov of Bulgaria was another star of the tournament. The balding midfielder possessed silky skills and great vision, and it was his headed goal which knocked Germany out in the quarter-finals. Hristo Stoitchkov and Krassimir Balakov also played a major part in Bulgaria's success.

The prospects in Eastern Europe look extremely healthy. Following the end of Communism, the best players from Eastern Europe are free to move to other European leagues and they are now reaping the benefits of this.

Half of the Bulgarian squad played outside their home country and eight Romanians graced foreign leagues prior to the World Cup.

Other Eastern European nations have also shown promise over the past twelve months. The Czech Republic defeated Ireland in Dublin last May, and Russia, with their full complement of players will be a match for anybody.

With nations like Belarus, Georgia and Ukraine entering competitions for the first time, the Eastern European uprising could be set to run and run.

One thing we now know for certain after USA '94 is that the established powers of the game from Western Europe and South America are no longer having it all their own way, and that is just one of the reasons USA '94 was such a success.

● 42-year-old Roger Miller became the oldest man to score in the finals when he grabbed Cameroon's consolation goal in their 6-1 drubbing by Russia.

● Nigeria's Rachidi Yekini puts Luca Marchegiani, Italy, under pressure.

● Gheorghe Hagi, Romania.

the Clothes Show

Some of the more colourful folk from World Cup '94

NORWAY

BRAZIL

COLOMBIA

ENERGIA SOLAR S.A.

12

NIGERIA

UNITED STATES

Perhaps the most colourful character of them all - Mexico's goalkeeper Jorge Campos.

CAMEROON

what do YOU remember about the World Cup?

SEE QUESTION 20

1. Which player scored the first goal of the World Cup Finals?

2. The Republic of Ireland kicked off their campaign with a shock win over Italy. In which stadium was the match played?

3. Which player broke a World Cup record by scoring five goals in one match?

4. Which star of the tournament also appeared in last season's Anglo-Italian Cup Final?

5. Ipswich Town, Norwich City, Motherwell, Derby County and Swindon Town each supplied one player in the Finals. Name them.

6. Which English club provided most World Cup players?

7. Who was the only goalkeeper to be sent off during the tournament?

8. Dutch striker Dennis Bergkamp was named after which footballing hero of the 1960s?

9. Which country failed to score a goal in the USA?

10. Which two players equalled the World Cup record of 21 World Cup Finals appearances?

11. Which countries were involved in the play-off for third and fourth place?

12. Which goalkeeper saved a penalty in normal play?

13. Which Italian player was banned for eight matches after using an elbow to break the nose of Spain's Luis Enrique?

14. Which country reached the semi-finals having never previously won a match in World Cup Finals?

15. Which country scored most goals in the Finals?

16. Which two players shared the distinction of being the top individual scorer?

17. Name either of the two British referees who were on duty during the competition.

18. Which German player was sent home from America following a breach of discipline?

19. Unfancied USA reached the last 16, but which Brazilian scored the goal which finally knocked them out?

20. Name the captain who lifted the trophy after his side won the Final.

ANSWERS

1. Jürgen Klinsmann in Germany's 1-0 victory over Bolivia.

2. The Giants Stadium, New York.

3. Oleg Salenko in Russia's 6-1 win over Cameroon.

4. Romanian captain Gheorghe Hagi, who played for Brescia against Notts County.

5. Boncho Guentchev (Bulgaria), Efan Ekoku (Nigeria), Tommy Coyne (Ireland), John Harkes (USA) and Jan-Aage Fjortoft (Norway).

6. Aston Villa (Paul McGrath, Steve Staunton, Ray Houghton and Andy Townsend).

7. Gianluca Pagliuca of Italy.

8. Despite the different spelling, it was former Manchester United and Scotland star, Denis Law.

9. Greece.

10. Diego Maradona (Argentina) and Lothar Matthäus (Germany).

11. Bulgaria and Sweden.

12. None. Every penalty was converted.

13. Mauro Tassotti.

14. Bulgaria.

15. Sweden (15 goals)

16. Hristo Stoitchkov (Bulgaria) and Oleg Salenko (Russia) with six goals each.

17. Philip Don (England); Les Mottram (Scotland).

18. Stefan Effenberg.

19. Bebeto.

20. Dunga (Brazil).

state hopping

SAN FRANCISCO

LOS ANGELES

DALLAS

CHICAGO

DETROIT

BOSTON

NEW YORK

WASHINGTON

ORLANDO

FIFTY-FOUR thousand miles in four weeks is enough to put off even the most hardy traveller, but that was the mileage clocked up by photographers Stewart Kendall and Richard Sellers when covering last summer's World Cup finals.

Plane-hopping between Orlando and Los Angeles, San Francisco and Dallas, Chicago and New York, Detroit and Washington, Stewart and Richard managed to take in 36 out of the 52 matches.

The hectic travelling schedule was amply rewarded by super matches, super stadia and the chance to photograph the world's top soccer stars.

"Every ground had its appeal," says Richard, "but the best for me was the Giants Stadium, New York, for its atmosphere — especially in the Italy-Republic of Ireland match.

"The facilities for us wherever we went were superb with courtesy buses laid on from airport to football ground.

"The only problem was early on when I nearly didn't get a pass for the opening match but it was "plane" sailing after that."

"Plane" being the operative word for both men spent quite a lot of time inside one!

In between flying and matches Stewart and Richard did find some time for sight-seeing, and rubbing shoulders with the big names of World football,like Eric Cantona.

And on their arrival back home as if jet-lag wasn't bad enough, they had thousands of negatives to sort out and file.

"We're both looking forward to the European Championships in 1996. One thing we WON'T miss will be the travelling!" says Stewart.

WHO'S THAT WITH RICHARD SELLERS?!

15

made to measure!

TERRY PHELAN was probably unique among the stars at the World Cup finals in the US last summer — he was the only one who buys his own football socks!

In fact, the Republic of Ireland left-back is also probably the only professional footballer in Britain who washes his own socks after matches.

Phelan has a secret. He has his own stock of football socks — for club and country.

He arrives for international matches for the Republic with his own socks, and takes them home afterwards. He also supplies his own pairs for Premier League games.

"I don't like most of the socks that are provided at international and club level," reveals Terry. "They are too tight.

"I have big calf muscles, and most socks are so tight at the top, they give me cramp. My whole game is based on my running, so to get cramp is a disaster.

"Also, modern football socks are very thick. I hate them. I don't like my boots to feel too tight.

"A pal of mine has a sports shop in Manchester. He supplies me with special socks that are loose at the top, and quite thin.

"I take a couple of pairs to international matches, and then take them home to wash.

"Mick McCarthy also used to have the same trouble with Ireland. He told me he had problems with tight socks giving him cramp at the World Cup finals in Italy.

"I have my own brand for club matches, which are looked after in the kit room. Sometimes I have to be careful I've got the right colour to go with our away strip. When Manchester City played in a purple away strip last season, that colour was hard to come by.

"I suppose it has become a bit of a superstition with me now. I will always feel happier providing my own socks."

BRYAN GUNN

NORWICH CITY

only the best

... SO SAYS ABERDEEN'S SCOTT BOOTH

● EOIN JESS — An ideal striking partner for Scott.

will do !

I spent my whole childhood dreaming of playing for my home town team, Aberdeen. Every week, my parents would follow me on my travels as I played for various boys' teams — I think they must have realised football would be my future.

Funnily enough, I was never the star player in those days — there was always a boy rated higher than me. One I remember was Shaun Rouse, later with Rangers, and also Darren Ferguson, son of Aberdeen's most successful boss, Alex, now manager of Manchester United.

There was only one team for us — Darren had even been a Pittodrie ballboy.

From about the age of 11, there was usually a scout from the Dons watching our progress.

At that time we played on gravel pitches, in the streets, just anywhere for a game.

Five years went by, and I was taken down south for a few trials with Nottingham Forest. But I knew that if the Dons didn't come in for me, I'd just have to go to them.

And that's exactly what I did. I turned up at Pittodrie and said I should be playing for them. After all, they'd had a good enough look at me over those five years!

After two weeks' wait, my dream came true. Ian Porterfield was the manager who signed me, but by the time I actually joined, Alex Smith had taken over.

That was good news because Alex always gave his younger players a chance. But even breaking into the reserves was difficult, and I spent a year toiling in youth sides and getting a run in the BP Cup.

Then, after a year in the second team, I came on as a sub against St Mirren for the first team. I remember one minute being frozen with nerves and the next minute just realising I was on the park and I had better make the most of it!

But my debut turned out perfectly, and I actually set up Charlie Nicholas for his last-ever goal for the club.

That game really stands out when I look back, but another special match was the Scottish Cup replay with Clydebank two seasons ago, when I scored twice in our 4-3 win.

I ended up top scorer in that competition, even though we once again went through the bitter disappointment of losing in the Final.

My first international for Scotland against Germany at Ibrox, on March 24, 1993, was the biggest game of my life. In that one, too, I was thinking, "there's no turning back" when I came on. You just have to relax and go for it, a bit like diving head first into a swimming pool!

Playing for your country is a huge honour for any player and, when I scored for Scotland against Estonia, I can't describe how proud I felt.

Unfortunately, last season wasn't great for me as I struggled to get into the side, with injuries being the main reason.

I have a contract which takes me to the end of this season, so I really do have to make a big impression.

But, sadly, I feel the game in Scotland has become poorer in quality over the past few years. Too many sides think it's enough just to be defensive and stop skilful players from performing.

They don't seem to realise that only leaves the fans bored and disappointed.

I feel strongly that changes ought to be made to the game. I'm not suggesting we should go for the mad razzmatazz of, say, American football or baseball, but we should make going to a match an enjoyable day out for families.

True, the result is the important thing to the teams, but people should be able to say they enjoyed the occasion even if their side lost.

It's our Number One sport and sometimes I think we don't make enough of it — we should highlight the skills and trickery of the entertaining players, that's what is best about football.

But, for the players themselves, football's the best job you could have.

At Aberdeen, the players are always the most important folk, and I think that explains why they always manage to find new young players, like myself and my fellow striker, Eoin Jess — youngsters in the north east know there's only one club to be with.

People have made a lot of how good Eoin and I are as a "twin strike force", but actually I don't feel we have had nearly enough games together.

I reckon strike partnerships need at least half a season to really start working well — like Mark Hateley and Mo Johnston needed at Ibrox — or even Mark and Ally McCoist.

In fact, I think if Eoin and I got more opportunities to play together, we'd really start banging in the goals.

Eoin is maybe more of an outside-the-box player who likes to put in crosses and set up goals, and I definitely see myself as an out-and-out centre-forward. There's nothing to beat scoring goals, and I'd much rather be up front than in the midfield.

But, even though he might feel he's not playing in his best position, a good professional just gets on with the particular job his manager gives him.

In fact, I am fascinated by managers and coaches working out tactics, systems and such like.

I can see myself going into coaching or management when I stop playing. I might seem very young to already be thinking so far into the future, but I like thinking and talking about the game.

And I'm so serious about my job that, when I'm not at Pittodrie, I try to lead quite a sensible, healthy life. I'm a bit of a homebird, and I'm always very careful about what I eat and drink.

One of my favourite pastimes is playing the piano — I like the classics, such as Mozart, Tchaikovsky and Vivaldi. Mind you, we've nearly got a full band at Aberdeen, as 'keeper Michael Watt is a guitarist and Lee Richardson plays the drums!

But mostly I just eat, sleep and drink football. I've found that the easier things are, the more you take them for granted — and then you become spoiled.

Football is just a job, although it's a good one with big rewards. But, like any job, you must always give it your best shot if you want to be successful.

"GLORY, GLORY

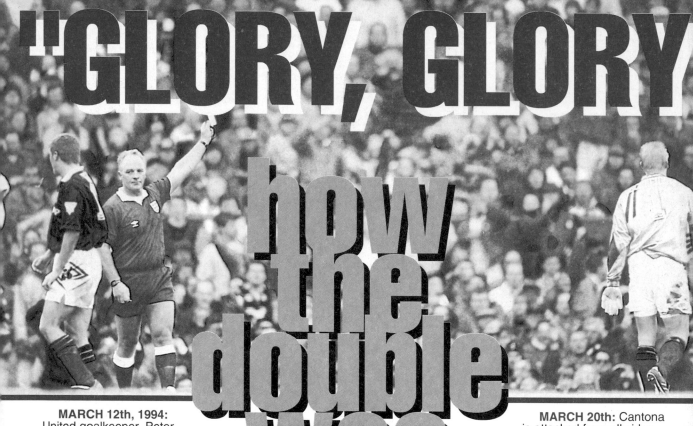

how the double was done !

MARCH 12th, 1994: United goalkeeper, Peter Schmeichel, is sent off against Charlton in the FA Cup quarter-final for deliberate handball outside the penalty area. United win 3-1, but Schmeichel's dismissal means he is suspended for the Coca-Cola Cup Final.

MARCH 13th: United draw Oldham in the FA Cup semi-final, but controversy rages over the venue for the game. The FA want to use Wembley, as do Oldham, but United want the game played nearer Manchester to prevent supporters having to pay for two Wembley games in two weeks.

MARCH 16th: Talk of United cracking under the pressure is banished with a 5-0 home league win over Sheffield Wednesday. It is United's biggest win over the Owls since 1907.

MARCH 17th: United's victory over Wednesday makes the bookmakers put them at evens for the treble. They are also 50-1 to win nothing.

MARCH 19th: A trip to bottom of the table Swindon Town turns into a nightmare for Alex Ferguson's side. While leading 2-1 thanks to goals from Roy Keane and Paul Ince, disaster strikes United. Eric Cantona is sent-off by referee Brian Hill for stamping on Swindon's John Moncur. Minutes later, Jan-Aage Fjortoft equalises for Swindon and United are lucky to escape with a draw.

MANCHESTER UNITED created history last season by becoming only the sixth team to win the League and FA Cup double. For this achievement, they will go down in history as one of the great sides of all-time.

For most of the season, United seemed to be coasting to success, but a series of controversies, defeats and media pressure put United off their stride and very nearly cost them everything.

This diary, which covers the last two months of their season, recalls the trails and tribulations United had to overcome to book their place in football history.

MARCH 20th: Cantona is attacked from all sides of the Media for his foul on Moncur and Alex Ferguson is under pressure to fine the Frenchman.

MARCH 22nd: Ferguson fines Cantona two weeks' wages for his sending-off, but things only get worse. United travel to Arsenal in a vital game for their championship hopes, but Cantona is sent-off again for two bookable offences.

Referee, Vic Callow, shows Cantona the red card in the 89th minute following a challenge on Arsenal's Tony Adams. Unlike his dismissal at Swindon, Cantona can count himself unfortunate to be dismissed following TV evidence.

Away from the controversy, United earn a valuable point against The Gunners with two goals from Lee Sharpe, who makes his first appearance since December.

MARCH 23rd: United, now only six points ahead of Blackburn who have a game in hand, are rocked by the news that Cantona will be suspended for five games. He will miss the vital game at Blackburn, plus the semi-final against Oldham.

Cantona's team-mate, Mark Hughes, speaks up for the widely condemned Frenchman, saying: "Eric is not happy. All he wants to do is play football. We are all behind him 100% because we know what he's done for this club."

MAN UNITED !!

MARCH 26th: Blackburn beat Swindon 3-1 and close the gap on United to three points.

MARCH 27th: United's desire to become the first team to win the domestic treble is ended by Aston Villa in the Coca-Cola Cup Final. Villa fully deserve their victory and United are left contemplating the fact they may yet end the season with nothing in the trophy cabinet. United, who have Les Sealey in goal for the suspended Schmeichel, score through Mark Hughes, but minutes later see Andrei Kanchelskis dismissed for deliberate handball.

Kanchelskis will miss the FA Cup semi-final, as will Roy Keane whose booking earns him a one-match ban.

MARCH 29th: Blackburn go to Wimbledon knowing a win will take them to the top of the table, but Wimbledon win 4-1 to give United the chance to open up a six point lead.

MARCH 30th: Six points is again United's lead following a 1-0 victory over traditional rivals, Liverpool. Paul Ince scores for United in Eric Cantona's last game before his ban commences, but controversy again surrounds United's victory. Referee Keith Hackett awards Liverpool a penalty, but changes his mind following a discussion with his linesman.

MARCH 31st: The bookmakers make United 1-8 to retain the title.

APRIL 2nd: United go to Ewood Park, Blackburn for their most important game of the season. Without Eric Cantona, United fail to make any impact and two goals from Alan Shearer give Rovers a 2-0 win to cut United's lead to 3 points. Manager, Alex Ferguson, promises changes for the next game against Oldham at Old Trafford.

CONTINUED OVERLEAF

21

"GLORY, GLORY MAN

APRIL 4th: Dion Dublin, United's forgotten man, comes off the bench to score a vital goal against local rivals, Oldham. United win 3-2 to maintain their lead over Blackburn who keep up the heat by trouncing Everton 3-0 at Goodison Park.

APRIL 10th: United travel to Wembley to play Oldham in the FA Cup semi-final, and come within a whisker of being knocked out. Neil Pointon gives Oldham the lead in the second half of extra time and The Latics appear to be on the way to the Cup Final, but Mark Hughes saves the day for United with a spectacular equaliser in the dying seconds.

The draw is good news for United as it means the vital game at Leeds has to be re-scheduled to accommodate the replay. Eric Cantona, named as the PFA Player of the Year, will now be available for the trip to Elland Road.

APRIL 11th: Blackburn defeat Aston Villa 1-0 at Ewood Park and go joint top with United.

APRIL 13th: Bryan Robson inspires United to a 4-1 victory in the semi-final replay over Oldham at Maine Road, Manchester. The returning Andrei Kanchelskis also stars, and the United fans chant 'Andrei must stay' in an effort to make the United management offer the Ukrainian a new contract after

hearing the winger is set to leave the club.

APRIL 16th: United remain top on goal difference, even though they lose 1-0 at Wimbledon. Blackburn, who played earlier, lose 3-1 at Southampton and fail to overtake United.

APRIL 23rd: Eric Cantona returns for United in the Manchester 'Derby' and scores twice to put United back on course for the championship. A 2-0 victory means United's lead at the top returns to 3 points.

APRIL 24th: Blackburn surprisingly fail to beat QPR following a late equaliser by Rangers defender, Karl Ready. United are now two points clear with a game in hand.

APRIL 27th: United win 2-0 at Leeds on the same night as Blackburn win 2-1 at West Ham. United now need only five points to retain the title.

MAY 1st: Ipswich Town surprise United by taking an early lead in their clash at Portman Road, but United fight back with goals from Cantona and Ryan Giggs to win 2-1. In a match marred by injuries to both teams, United have 'keeper Peter Schmeichel carried off with an injured right ankle. He looks set to miss the FA Cup Final.

UNITED!"

MAY 2nd: Coventry City's Julian Darby scores twice to end Blackburn's title challenge in a 2-1 defeat for Kenny Dalglish's side. United are champions again and face two more games knowing their fate is already decided.

May 4th: United beat Southampton 2-0 at Old Trafford to set a new points record for the championship with 91 points.

MAY 8th: A packed Old Trafford sees United lift the Premier League trophy again following a 0-0 draw with Coventry. United finish on 92 points, eight points clear of Blackburn. The game also sees the end of Bryan Robson's Manchester United career — he plays his last game for United before leaving the club to take the player-manager's job at First Division Middlesbrough.

MAY 14th: United face Chelsea in the FA Cup Final with a fit Peter Schmeichel and, after a slow start, run in four goals to become only the fourth team this century to do the 'Double'. Eric Cantona makes history by scoring two penalties, and Mark Hughes and Brian McClair finish the scoring.

Steve Bruce creates history, as he is the first Englishman this century to captain a double-winning side. The result is cruel on Chelsea, who dominated for long periods, and hit the crossbar through Gavin Peacock. The 4-0 scoreline is the second biggest Cup Final winning margin of all-time.

MAY 15th: United parade through Manchester with the FA Cup and FA Carling Premiership trophy.

THE GUNNE MUSEU OF M

ORIGINS

THE EARLY YEARS 1886 1925

Arsenal Football Club owes its origins to a group of young Scots who worked at the Woolwich Arsenal.

Like many who came to earn a living there, these young men felt out of place in the home counties, where rugby and cricket were the popular games of the late Victorian age. Led by David Danskin, they founded Dial Square Football Club, named after the part of the Arsenal in which most of them worked.

The club took subscriptions of 6d (2½p) from 15 men, while Danskin himself paid 3s (15p), a tenth of his weekly wage. The money was used to buy a ball.

Dial Square FC played their first game on 11 December 1886 when they defeated Eastern Wanderers 6-0 at a ground on the Isle of Dogs.

The Arsenal team of 1890

● How the club began . . .

TRIUMPHS OF THE 1930s

● Curator Ian Cook, with the museum's tribute to the 1930's. In the glass case is the autographed ball from the 1936 F.A. Cup Final.

● Well-lit displays and wide passageways make viewing easy.

● Scotland legend Alex James figures prominently in the display. Here are his shirts from the 1936 Final and a Scotland cap from the famous "Wembley Wizards" game of 1928. James scored twice in Scotland's 5-1 win over England.

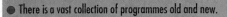
● There is a vast collection of programmes old and new.

RS' M EMORIES

● Over the years, Arsenal have won more than their fair share of silverware. The museum houses replicas of F.A. Cup, League Cup and Barclay's League triumphs, while room was found for their latest "catch" — the Cup Winners' Cup!

● Championship medals won by Charlie George and Peter Storey in the famous "double-winning" season of 1970-71.

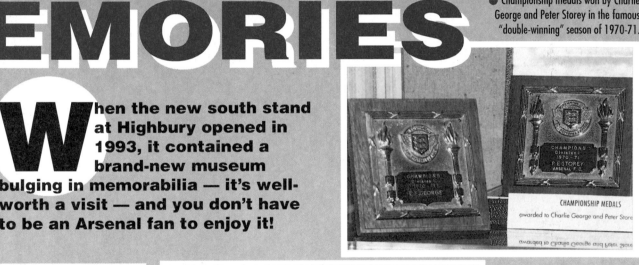

CHAMPIONSHIP MEDALS
awarded to Charlie George and Peter Store

When the new south stand at Highbury opened in 1993, it contained a brand-new museum bulging in memorabilia — it's well-worth a visit — and you don't have to be an Arsenal fan to enjoy it!

● For those wanting a quicker run through Arsenal's history there is the computerised "Arsenal Archive".

● It's not only the men's team that did well! In season 1992-93 the Arsenal ladies team won the lot — F.A. Cup, League Cup AND League.

● Greeting you as you come in is a "cannibalised" bus (chassis and wheels removed). This was used to show off the championship and cup trophies in 1989, 1991 and 1993.

anch aw

A LIFE ON THE OCEAN WAVES BECKONS FOR SHEFFIELD UNITED'S **GLYN HODGES!**

ors eigh !

Carl Bradshaw

SHEFFIELD UNITED playmaker Glyn Hodges may opt for a life on the High Seas when the tide eventually goes out on his football career.

It would seem a suitable career move for the 29-year-old midfielder who spent several seasons helping Sheffield United steer clear of the tricky waters at the foot of the Premiership.

Last year he enrolled on a Marine Navigation course at a local college and that will enable him to be equally at home on the ocean waves as the Bramall Lane pitch.

Glyn tells me, "My interest in Marine Navigation was sparked off after a terrible land holiday in Spain. It was the worst holiday I ever had.

"I didn't enjoy the hotel we stayed at and on top of that my mother-in-law came back with food poisoning. She was ill for several months.

"On the way back from Spain I was speaking to a lady on the plane. She had spent her holiday with her husband on their yacht in the Mediterranean. They had started off in France and sailed down the coast. She had to catch a flight home and left her husband to sail round to Italy.

"I thought it was very independent and exciting and conjured up images of life on the ocean waves. After the experiences I'd just suffered, such a holiday really appealed to me.

"I asked how I go about planning such a holiday. I thought it was just a matter of getting my sea legs, but she suggested I should learn something about navigation. That meant sitting a navigation course.

"Soon afterwards, I had this fellow in to plumb my bathroom. He told me some marvellous stories of the time he was sent to a diving school in the Black Sea. But it was

something he told me later on which really grabbed my attention . He had previously been self-employed and sailed boats from England to America for wealthy customers. That really appeals to me.

"I mentioned my interest and he told me that Stradbrook College in Sheffield runs a navigation course.

"The first couple of weeks on the course went as well as I could have expected. But I've got no practical experience of sailing and soon found it got quite technical.

"I found that I couldn't really afford to miss a week because I would have had so much work to catch up on.

"But that proved to be the case, particularly when it came to sitting the exams. I did well in the first written exam, but I had problems fitting in the second exam.

"It was to take place right at the end of the season. It couldn't have been a worse time, particularly with United in the relegation battle.

"For instance, on the week I was to sit the second exam, I was playing for the reserves. The next week we were playing Oldham Athletic and the following week we were in Australia.

"I also didn't have too much spare time to do revision. Thankfully, the exams covered all the key points I'd studied. There were questions on plotting fixes on a map, even questions on what ropes to attach to the anchor.

"I passed the written exams then went on a five-day continuous practical at the end of the course. My only fear was being seasick and never setting foot on a boat again.

"I've not been able to rope in any of my United team-mates to do the course, though I might have persuaded Carl Bradshaw, before his move to Norwich during the summer.

"Carl's father has done the course and qualified. He has a yacht

and Carl spent his honeymoon on it in Majorca.

"He was unable to take the yacht out to sea because he wasn't qualified and I think that's a bit of a shame. I think he regrets not being able to go out on it.

"I tried to get Carl involved in the course but he was reluctant at the time and in the end it was too late to enrol.

"I'm keeping my eye open for a yacht or a motor cruiser if everything goes according to plan.

"However, it's an expensive hobby. It might be a case of waiting until I win the Pools. I might just charter a 6-8 berth yacht, so I can spread the cost.

"All the lads at Bramall Lane are saying that I should do something that will help me after my football career, but their idea of the sort of courses to do is different to mine.

"A few players do accountancy, and other business courses, but that's too much like going back to school.

"I've got a low tolerance threshold. My concentration can wane very easily and I can get easily bored. But I enjoy the navigation course.

"However, my union, the Professional Football Association, see the merits in my course. They have paid 75 per cent of its cost.

"The union have always worried what happens to players if they get injured tomorrow and their career is ended.

"I'll give you a typical example of what I mean. There is one young player at Bramall Lane who was at college full-time doing a high-brow course. He joined United and now doesn't want to go back to college and complete his course.

"I know you can't put an old head on young shoulders, but I've said to him to carry on with his studies. It's important to have something to fall back on after a player's career is over."

something

TOO MANY DOUBTERS FOR NOTTINGHAM FOREST'S **STAN COLLYMORE**

IT was after my first few months at Forest that rumours about my temperament began to spread.

People began to say that I couldn't handle the big games, that my attitude was suspect and that I just used to go missing when the pressure was on. It was all a load of rubbish.

It started when Forest played Sheffield Wednesday in a cup match back in January 1994. It was billed as the return of Forest's former star, Des Walker, to the City Ground to face Stan Collymore. When I didn't play in that game everyone assumed that I had ducked out and that I was frightened, which wasn't the case.

From that game on, the speculation just grew and grew, even though I knew that I would face any team, anywhere and at any time.

It was not a matter of me not wanting to play but a case of not being able to do so. I was forced to miss 23 games last season because of injury. I had to miss the first month through tonsilitis and then I had a hamstring tear, so all the games I missed were because of legitimate reasons and not because I was scared of playing in the big matches.

I think that I was able to lay those rumours to rest in the games at the end of that season because I was in the thick of the action when we had to play crucial matches against close rivals Millwall and Derby County.

The Derby game in particular was a big, big game for a variety of reasons. If they had beaten us that night they could have been breathing down our necks with only a few weeks of the season left. On top of that, there was the pressure of it being a local derby where the feelings were really running high.

We won 2-0 and I felt that I played at the top of my form. Even the boss, Frank Clark, commented that it was my best away performance for Forest.

The fact that I played so well, even though I didn't get on the score sheet, and I did it against a £2.5 million player in Craig Short, proved to everyone that I can handle anything.

After all, the challenge of playing against the best is the reason that I'm in the game and the experience I've gained this year by doing that is something that I feel I've needed.

I think that people tend to forget that this is only my third full season of professional football and my first in the top division, so things are still new to me.

I played a couple of seasons in the First Division and I got to know all the centre-halves well and vice versa. So it has been nice to come up against opponents who haven't the same knowledge of me. To say that I don't relish playing against the top sides is totally untrue.

That wasn't the only rumour that was flying about. People also said that I was a lone striker and couldn't link up with somebody else, but that has never been the case.

I did play the majority of the games last year up on my own but that was not because the manager felt that I could only operate that way. It was a case of it being the only option open to the team.

We were struggling injury-wise during the early part of that season and Frank decided to counteract that by playing five across the middle and only myself up front. The plan was that when the ball was played to me, one of the midfield players would join me. It seemed to work really well, so we stuck at it.

I didn't mind playing there and I think that I have the game to do that job. I've always felt comfortable playing with my back to goal and I'm happy doing that. Sometimes it can be difficult because some of the passes you receive from your team-mates can only be flicked on and, with nobody there to help out, you can look a bit silly.

However, that doesn't mean that I'm unable to play in any other style. I've had striking partners before and never had a problem.

When I was at Southend, I formed a partnership with Brett Angell and we fed off each other superbly. Even last season I had a few games alongside Jason Lee without any problems whatsoever. In fact, I don't mind playing with one person up front or five!

I feel that I've proved those doubters wrong and hopefully this season will also have proved to Crystal Palace that they should not have let me go to Southend so cheaply a couple of years ago.

The nicest part of last year's promotion was that Crystal Palace also managed to get up. I know a few of the lads from my time there and I still keep in touch with them. I was really pleased for their manager, Alan Smith, because he is a nice bloke.

It is nice that we will continue to play Palace because last season I didn't play well when we went to Selhurst Park. It was my first game back after a lay-off and I wasn't fully fit, so I've been looking forward to going down there in the peak of fitness and raring to go.

to prove !

COURTESY OF
LANCASHIRE
EVENING POST

HOME . . .

FANFARE — That's what's dished up at Preston North End matches every other Saturday. Visitors to Deepdale are amazed when the Preston band strikes up on the terracing.

mak

COURTESY OF
SHEFFIELD STAR

BUGLE BOY — Sheffield Wednesday have bugler John Hemmingham to thank for making sure each game ends on a high note!

ing music

Sometimes there's as much playing OFF the pitch as on it!

IN THE MOOD — The man who orchestrates things in midfield for East Stirling is Glenn Miller. Glenn, an ex-student of the trombone, is pictured here with an album of his most famous namesake.

This is how United States star Alexi Lalas relaxes before a big match.

GAVIN PEACOCK   **CHELSEA**

X WORD

SEE 8 DOWN

CLUES ACROSS

6. The Lilywhites from Deepdale (7)
7. Elton John's favourite club (7)
9. International player's award (3)
10. Final score read-out (7)
11. How a wet strip feels (4)
12. Prevent a goal (4)
15. This David plays for Coventry (6)
17. Press account of a match (6)
18. Leicester City's nickname (5)
20. The penalty ——. (4)
23. Postal address of 8 Down (5, 6, 4)
25. See 2 down.
26. Former Premier League Boss, Bobby (5)
28. Goals could be scored direct from this (6)
30. Do Chelsea use this to cross Stamford? (6)
31. Team-_ _ _ _ (4)
33. Stingers from Brentford (4)
35. Does this Earl "Lord" it at Villa Park? (7)
36. Newcastle's Robert (3)
38. Main match official (7)
39. Team captain (7)

14. Could noisy supporters cause this? (7)
16. Wingers should be good at this (8)
19. Walsall fans on horse-back? (8)
21. Ex-Manchester City manager, Mr Allison (7)
22. We hope the ball ends up in here! (4-3)
24. Individual teams (5)
27. He may be guilty of a foul (8)
29. They are also known as Bristol Rovers (7)
32. A West-Country team (6)
34. First Division potters (5)
37. A study for Millwall? (3)

CLUES DOWN

1. Team entrance tests (6)
2. and 25 across. This is home for Sunderland (5, 4)
3. You will not be doing this on a football pitch! (7)
4. You would be, if you got a red card (3)
5. They play at Prenton Park (8)
8. Bradley Allen plays for them (6, 4, 7)
11. County of 32 down (5)
13. Show approval of a goal (7)

33

IN AT THE DEEP END !

● Here we go! Here we go! Here we go!
Garry arrives at Ibrox ready and willing for his first taste of taking part in top-class football.

The "Topical Times" arranged for Garry Fraser to spend a morning training with Glasgow Rangers. Easy going? Don't you believe it! . . .

● Easy going — so far! Clydesdale Cricket Ground . . . and under the watchful eyes of coaches Billy Kirkwood and John McGregor, the players start their training session — a gentle (?) jog round the park. Garry (third right) isn't last — yet!

● One-touch "Toro". Two players in the middle of a circle have to intercept passes from the others. Hard going. Garry touched the ball at least twice!

● Now for the hard stuff — a succession of 100 metre sprints, the players split into teams of four. A tentative Garry surveys his fellow sprinters — Mark Hateley, David Hagen and Neil Murray.

● Garry ends a creditable last — every time! If he hadn't been feeling the pace, he was now!

● While the players started a full-scale practice match, Garry decided to look in on a goalies' coaching session by Alan Hodgkinson for five young hopefuls, Neil Inglis, Colin Scott, Andrew Caldwell, Ian McFarlane and Stuart McIntosh. Plenty time to pose for the photographer (and catch some breath!)

● Let's see if I can get THIS one on target!

● Then, a word with manager Walter Smith:—
"We'd like you to do a job for the first team, Garry!"
"You WOULD?"
"Yes — go and run their baths!"

● Back to Ibrox for a well-earned shower and a bite to eat in the players' restaurant. Does he look as if he's glad it's all over?!

Our thanks to all at Ibrox particularly Walter Smith, Billy Kirkwood and John McGregor. Also to the players for their patience and tolerance. A final thought from Garry . . .
"I think I'll stick to watching football rather than playing it!"

FOOTBALL fans up and down the country are all proud of their own team in some way or another.

Newcastle United fans pride themselves on their huge 'Toon Army' banner, Queen's Park supporters constantly remind people that they play at the biggest ground in Scotland, and Wimbledon are famed for their 'Crazy Gang' spirit.

None of those claims to fame can match that of Blackburn Rovers though! How many clubs can say they have their very own radio station?

Blackburn stole a march on more glamorous clubs like Manchester United, Liverpool and Rangers.

When 'Radio Rovers' went on air for the first time back in October 1993, it was the first of its kind in Europe for a football club, and everybody connected with the club is rightly proud of their ground-breaking move into radio broadcasting.

Radio Rovers was set-up by radio broadcaster Alan Yardley following the initial idea of Mel Highmore, Rovers' Safety Officer, who felt a club of Blackburn's stature needed an improved system of public announcement for the benefit of supporters, himself and his team of stewards.

Alan Yardley reveals the story behind Radio Rovers.

"Ever since the beginning of the 1992/93 season there has been a team at Ewood Park manning the PA system, putting out a radio programme over the tannoy, "Alan explains.

"Even at that stage, before we actually became a radio station, we were approaching the matchday entertainment differently from most other clubs in that we were doing little things such as dedications and player interviews over the tannoy.

"That way was all well and good for the supporters inside Ewood Park, but for those fans outside the ground or those who were unable to get to the game, they were missing out, so that was one of the reasons we decided to apply for a broadcasting licence.

"There were, of course, other considerations for us to widen our range. Radio Rovers can offer vital information in terms of safety to our supporters and that was probably the prime reason for Mel Highmore to come up with the idea.

"By being able to reach so many people we can warn them of possible traffic problems near Ewood, ticket availability, crowd congestion, and in some cases, news of postponements at the ground.

"Good communication is vital when you have around 20,000 people approaching one venue such as Ewood Park and we feel our service is something which is perhaps long overdue.

"With the full co-operation of the Police at Blackburn, we feel our service to the fans in terms of information is vital."

Everybody involved at Radio Rovers will agree the communication aspect of the programme is the most important part, however, the other area of the production which provides the entertainment is the aspect which makes Radio Rovers stand out from the rest.

"We are in a very fortunate position at Radio Rovers because we know who our audience is and we can cater specifically for them," Alan goes on.

"Because of this we can unashamedly design our programme for their needs and place the emphasis on Blackburn Rovers. An example of this is our match-by-match series called 'Rhythms of The Blues.'

"On Rhythms of The Blues, we ask a different player every week to name his five favourite records, which we play for him, and also our reporter, Wendy Howard, does an interview with the player which we use in between each record.

"The interview is usually personal and it allows the supporters to learn more about their favourite players.

"Playing their favourite records can sometimes be a bit painful! Their taste in records is a bit strange to say the least.

"Colin Hendry is a good example of bizarre tastes. His selection consisted of AC/DC, Bryan Adams and a bagpipe version of Amazing Grace!

"We're just waiting for Kevin Moran to choose something like 'First Cut is the Deepest', or Alan Shearer to pick 'Keep On Running!'

"Having such a good accessibility to the players means we can bring all the latest news to our listeners straight away and that gives us a lead over the other radio stations in our area.

"As we only broadcast on matchdays we have to make sure our production is good enough to make the listeners tune in whenever we have a game. If they tune into 1413 AM during the week they won't get anything.

"This means we have to make sure they want to come back to us on matchdays by putting out a quality production every week.

"I'm convinced we are doing this and I think Radio Rovers will continue to go from strength to strength."

● Colin Hendry — a man of many tastes!

● (Above) Blackburn Rovers' Safety Officer Mel Highmore.
● Alan Yardley (right) with his Radio Rovers team of Gerald Jackson, presenter, and Wendy Howard, reporter.

PUZZLE

REVOLVER

Solve the clues from 1 to 12. All answers are 6 letters long, with a football connection, and should be entered from outer to inner. The twelve shaded squares reading from 1 to 12 spell a football ground.

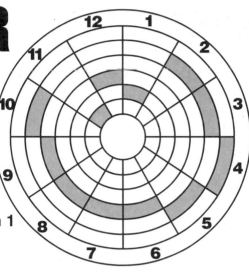

CLUES
1. CONTROL
2. FOOTBALL
3. CROSS FROM A DEAD-BALL
4. PROTECT
5. BOOTED
6. OVERTOOK
7. GETS A GOAL
8. VICTOR
9. ELIMINATION CONTEST (3,3)
10. OLD-FASHIONED TERRACING NOISE-MAKER!
11. GOAL SCORED WITHOUT KICKING
12. INTERCEPT AT FOOTBALL

SIX OF THE BEST

Identify the six footballers, then fill in the grid with the christian names and surnames. Next put the numbered letters in the corresponding numbered boxes to find the name of a football club.

TIME

SCRAMBLER

Unscramble the jumbled letters to make 8 football clubs.(6 English & 2 Scottish). Then rearrange the shaded letters to make another football club.

#	Grid	Clue
1	F U L H A M	**1 LAFHUM**
2	A R S A N E L	**2 NELASRA**
3	L E E D S	**3 ESLDE**
4	C H E L S E A	**4 HECASEL**
5	S T O K E	**5 TKSEO**
6	R A I T H	**6 AIRTH**
7	I P S W I C H	**7 HWCISIP**
8	P A R T I C K	**8 CKATPIR**

PUZZLE TIME ANSWERS ON PAGE 124

STAR FILLING

Fit the 6 names into the grid, so the centre column reveals the surname of one of the names across. (Footballer)

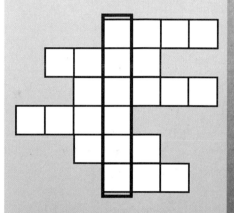

**ALAN   BILL   BRIAN
DES   JOHN   SID**

FLY THE FLAG

Fill the grid with football words reading down. If correct a football manager should appear across the centre, and the shaded squares when sorted, the club he manages.

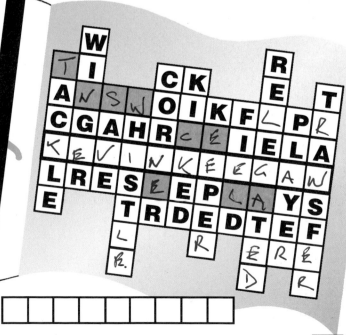

39

GORDAN PETRIC　　　　　**DUNDEE UNITED**

ROBBIE FOWLER   **LIVERPOOL**

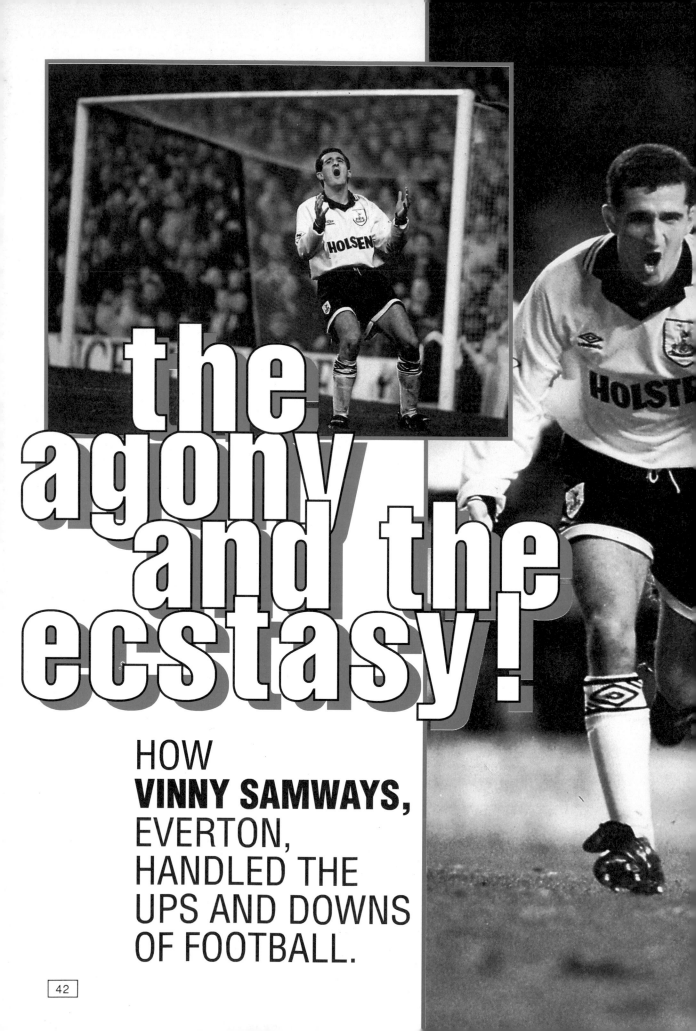

the agony and the ecstasy!

HOW
VINNY SAMWAYS,
EVERTON,
HANDLED THE
UPS AND DOWNS
OF FOOTBALL.

VINNY SAMWAYS

VINNY SAMWAYS endured the toughest afternoon of his playing career last season — but survived the experience to become a better player.

The Spurs midfield player hit the low point of his life in a nightmare home defeat. Vinny gifted a goal to opponents Sheffield Wednesday, who went on to win 3-1, pushing Tottenham deeper into relegation trouble.

For the rest of the match, Samways was cruelly, and unmercifully, booed by a section of the White Hart Lane crowd. It would have been enough to destroy many players.

Indeed, in the same situation, most managers would have substituted a player given so much abuse by his own fans.

But not Spurs team boss Ossie Ardiles. He saw the positive side of keeping Samways in the action.

And in the end, the nightmare of that day turned into one of the highlights of Vinny's seven-year career at Tottenham.

Now the Londoner believes the incident could have been a major turning point in his career.

"I deserved to get some stick that day. I made a bad mistake, and gave away a goal," admits Samways. "But the reaction from the fans was a bit upsetting.

● Positive thinking from former manager Ossie Ardiles.

"When they started booing me, I didn't know what to do with myself. But I was determined not to let it affect me on the field.

"The manager could have taken me off, but he stuck by me. I feel that was the best thing he could have done.

"Afterwards, Ossie said the incident would be the making of me as a player. He was pleased because I showed a lot of character in carrying on playing normally, and not trying to 'hide'.

"I just had to ignore all the stick, and get on with the game. I didn't enjoy it, but that's football. The fans pay their money, and are entitled to their opinions.

"But afterwards, you wouldn't believe the kind of support I had from genuine fans. I've never had so many letters in my life, all saying how sorry people were for what happened.

"I've kept every letter. I'll never throw them out. They showed me just how much the supporters really do care about the players at Spurs.

"Receiving the letters was very rewarding for me. If ever I get a bit down, I take them out and read a few.

"They really mean a lot to me. I'm a local lad, and Spurs were always my team.

"I feel the whole episode proves I can handle the ups and downs of football. It has made me stronger in myself.

"In the past, people have knocked Spurs for not showing enough character. I believe we do have it, but maybe it takes something like that to realise it yourself.

"Last season was a tough one for the club. We obviously struggled, and you can't blame the supporters for getting upset.

"I hope we've now put it all behind us."

Following the departure of previous manager Terry Venables, Samways was unsettled at White Hart Lane — until the arrival of Ossie Ardiles.

The Argentinian star had been a major influence on Vinny when he was a ground staff youngster. One of Vinny's greatest memories was playing in Ossie's testimonial match.

"I was only 17 at the time, and just a youth team player." he recalls. "I came on as a substitute in the match against Inter Milan.

"Glenn Hoddle and Ossie were in midfield, and Diego Maradona was a guest player on the night. It's a brilliant memory for me.

"The whole evening was superb. I was in there with three of the best players in the world.

"There was a lot of uncertainty about the future after the departure of Terry Venables as manager. Nobody knew what was happening, and I was a bit unsettled.

"Ossie's arrival changed all that. He has a great appreciation of how the game should be played.

"His kind of football is the sort I enjoy. He likes to play out from the back."

However, last season ended on a sour note with Spurs receiving a hefty FA punishment for off-field indiscretions – a move which shocked all the players.

"I was gutted. It has made things very hard for the club this season."

But after his problems at Tottenham last season, twenty-six-year-old Vinny is now looking forward to the best years of his career, and has made a completely fresh start at Mike Walker's Everton, after a £2.2 million close-season move.

Those fan letters proved to Vinny that he has the strength of character to put his nightmare behind him, and keep alive his hopes of international football.

9 game night

UNTIL transfer deadline day last season, Anders Limpar had no idea that his campaign was going to be transformed so radically.

One minute, the Swedish international winger was playing out the season in a low-key role with Arsenal, feeling a bit left out as his club-mates headed towards European Cup Winners' Cup glory and worrying about his chances of playing in the World Cup Finals.

The next, he was heading for Merseyside to complete a surprise move to Everton, which plunged him straight into a desperate relegation battle.

But that was only the first surprise for Limpar. Even after signing for manager Mike Walker, he never imagined that he was destined to play a central role in the most dramatic day of the Premiership season.

By the time the final day of the League campaign arrived, Limpar's new club had slumped into the bottom three having won just five points from his first eight matches.

Everton knew they had to win their last fixture and hope that one of the three clubs immediately above them dropped points.

Visitors to Goodison that day were the 'Crazy Gang' from Wimbledon and the Premiership's form side, undefeated in nine matches and the last opponents anyone would want as they battled for survival.

Needing a win to give themselves a chance of finishing in their highest-ever League position, the Dons had been promised an all-expenses paid trip to Las Vegas by Chairman Sam Hammam if they took the three points which would consign Everton to the First Division for the first time in 40 years.

Wimbledon arrived at the ground fired up after their team coach had been set ablaze during the night while parked outside their hotel headquarters.

mare...

And things immediately began going wrong for Everton, with Limpar cast as the early villain. After just four minutes, he handled the ball in his own penalty area and Dean Holdsworth converted the spot-kick.

After 20 minutes, Gary Ablett diverted the ball into his own net to put Wimbledon two ahead, and Everton looked doomed.

Four minutes later, however, Limpar was in the thick of the drama again, as he controversially tumbled in the Wimbledon penalty box to earn a penalty for his own side, to the disbelief of visiting defender Peter Fear, who appeared to have stood off his opponent.

That moment sparked off the most amazing comeback as Graham Stuart scored from the spot and Everton hauled back the deficit to win 3-2, securing their place in the Premiership with just nine minutes to spare, amid scenes of wild jubilation at Goodison.

Though it was such a close shave, however, Limpar looks back on the whole episode as a much-needed shot in the arm for his career.

He says, "It was well-known that I'd been having problems at Arsenal, so it wasn't a hard decision to agree a move to Everton.

"I hadn't been playing regularly for Highbury manager George Graham and felt pretty sure that, even if Arsenal went all the way to the final of the Cup Winners' Cup

● The Great Escape! Everton celebrate the goal that kept them in the Premiership

BUT THERE WAS A HAPPY ENDING FOR EVERTON'S ANDERS LIMPAR

(which they eventually won), I probably wouldn't be involved.

"All the same, I was surprised when I was suddenly made available at the time of the transfer deadline. Though I suspected my time was running out at the club, I thought they would keep me until the end of the season and use me in the occasional Premiership match just to cover for other players who were involved in the European run.

"But I was very pleased when the opportunity of a transfer came along. I had a choice of Manchester City or Everton, and opted for the latter.

"The main thing that had worried me was my chance of playing for Sweden in the World Cup Finals.

"You need to be playing hard, competitive football in order to keep yourself fit for such an event.

"Being involved in a relegation battle with Everton provided me with exactly that sort of preparation, although I had gone through most of the season not expecting to end the campaign battling to help my club stay in the Premier League.

"But I knew this was too great a club to go down to the First Division. Although that is exactly what everybody said about Nottingham Forest a year earlier as they headed towards relegation, I was convinced it wouldn't happen to Everton. We

had too many good players to lose out."

With survival assured after that dramatic last day, Limpar was able to relax and concentrate on the greater things he hopes to achieve with Everton, having signed a three-year-contract with the club.

He is also able to reflect on the irony that he began playing professional football on Merseyside seven years late, having been denied the chance to sign for arch rivals Liverpool as a youngster, because of red tape.

Anders recalls, "I had been playing really good football with my club, Orgryte, which is based in Gothenburg. I was also becoming very ambitious and hoped to attract the interest of one of the big clubs in England, France or Germany.

"So when Liverpool asked me to train with them for a week, with a view to signing, it was a great opportunity for me.

"At that time, in the autumn of 1986, Liverpool and Everton were certainly the best two sides in England. Kenny Dalglish was the manager at Anfield, which was another big attraction for me.

"At the end of my week, he told me that he wanted me to sign on. It was the big chance I wanted and, of course, I would have signed immediately.

"But then came the big blow when I was told that I couldn't stay, because I would not be granted a work permit.

"Because Sweden was not a member of the European Community, the rules stated that I needed to have won ten international caps before I could play for an English club. I wasn't an international player then, so I had to give up my dream for the time being.

"It was a terrible disappointment to have to return to Sweden after having my hopes built up so much. Liverpool were one of the best sides in Europe and to have come so close to playing for them, then been let down by bureaucracy, was a tremendous blow.

"However, once I'd recovered from the initial disappointment, the episode actually helped me. When I started playing for Orgryte again, I found that my confidence had been given such a big lift because Liverpool had shown that interest in me.

"I was bouncing all the way through that winter and my form was better than it had ever been. I made my debut for Sweden in April 1987 and quickly established myself as a regular in the national side.

"So although I am now determined to be successful with Everton and help them reach the top, I can still look back and thank Liverpool for giving me that early boost."

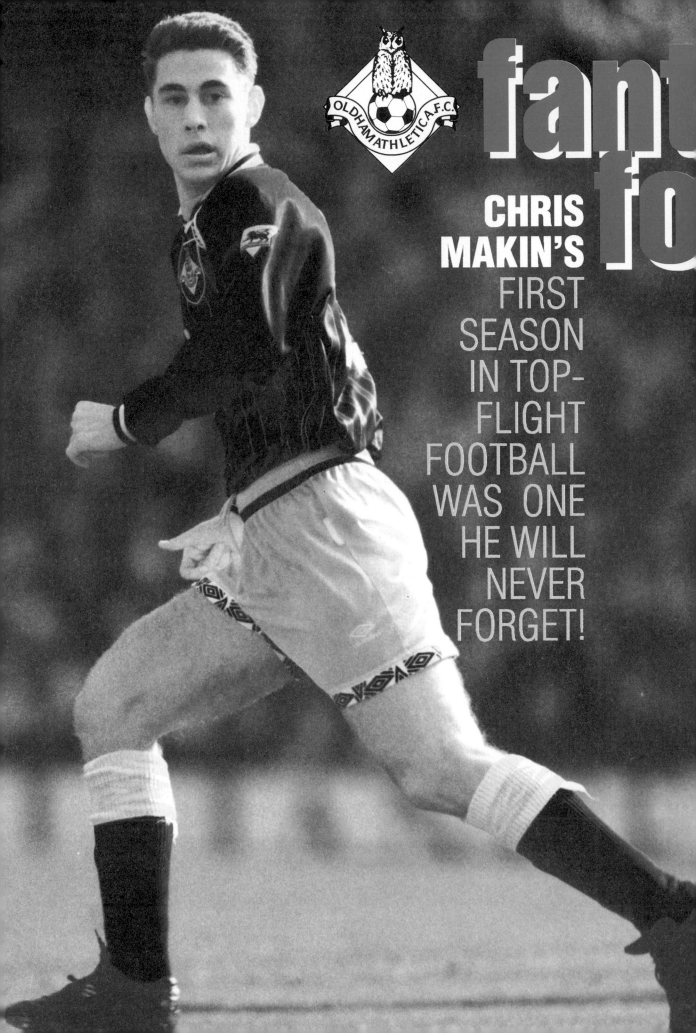

fant
fo

CHRIS MAKIN'S FIRST SEASON IN TOP-FLIGHT FOOTBALL WAS ONE HE WILL NEVER FORGET!

asy otball !

CHRIS MAKIN's first season in league football with Oldham Athletic last year was eventful to say the very least! If it was a storyline in a 'Roy Of The Rovers' comic, you would probably dismiss it as nonsense, thinking it would never happen in real life.

For Makin, though, the unbelievable story came true. In his first season in the top flight he found himself sent-off twice, called up for England Under-21s and in a Wembley semi-final against the team he supported fanatically as a boy, Manchester United.

Even more remarkable is the fact that all of this would never have happened if the 21-year-old defender hadn't picked up a bout of shingles while on loan at Third Division Preston North End!

Chris takes up the story, "If somebody had told me what lay ahead for me in my maiden season in first team football, I would never have believed them. I had an amazing season. One minute I'd be feeling really low, the next I'd be totally elated.

"Nobody expects so much to happen to them in one season, especially when it is your first. It could all have been so different though, because if I hadn't caught shingles I would probably have signed for Preston.

"I had gone there at the start of the season on loan with a view to a permanent move. At the time I felt I was ready to leave Oldham and look elsewhere for first-team football.

"I had already spent three months on loan at Wigan Athletic at the end of the previous season and it gave me a taste for first-team football and I felt I would have to leave Boundary Park to get it.

"The move to Preston seemed a good one, and I was prepared to give it my best shot and try to win a contract. After two weeks there, however, I caught shingles and had no option but to return to Oldham because I was no use to the people at Preston.

"It took me a couple of weeks to get over the shingles, and I was ready to go back to Preston, but there was a bit of an injury crisis at Oldham and the manager, Joe Royle, put me in the side to face Arsenal.

"Both Andy Barlow and Neil Pointon were out so I was given my chance. It was just unfortunate that things went a bit wrong for me over the next couple of weeks.

"I was sent off at West Ham, but I thought it would be a one-off and put it down to experience. However, I was dismissed again the following Saturday at home to

● Wembley. Oldham v. Manchester United. A highlight for Chris.

Norwich. Television evidence showed I was unlucky to be sent off both times, but it wasn't really a consolation, I was still banned for four games.

"I felt pretty low at the time because I just couldn't believe what had hit me. In the Norwich game I had scored my first ever League goal, but was soon brought down to earth with the red card. I thought I was jinxed.

"Fortunately, manager Joe Royle kept his faith in me and he put me straight back into the side when my ban ended. It was the lift I needed after the month I had just had."

In true 'Roy Of The Rovers' style, things began to improve for Chris and the nightmare start to his Oldham career began to be put in the shade by his performances for his relegation-threatened team.

In March, he was called into the England Under-21 side for the game against Denmark, and although he didn't play, Chris saw it as a sign that things were getting better for him.

He continues, "It was a surprise to be called into the England squad and when I made my debut against Russia in May, it went a long way to making up for the start I made.

"The highlight, though, was playing against Manchester United twice in a period of six days. I used to go to as many of their games as I could and to play against them at Old Trafford and Wembley was a dream come true.

"I remember seeing them beat Barcelona 3-0 in front of 58,000 at Old Trafford in the European Cup Winners' Cup. United were 2-0 down from the first leg and given no chance, but Bryan Robson scored twice to equalise, and when Frank Stapleton hit the winner the place went wild. It was a fantastic occasion and the atmosphere was something I'd love to experience during my career.

"With my luck, you never know what could happen. If I look back in ten years' time, I'll be surprised if I have such an eventful season again.

"You go into every season wondering what lies ahead, but if I have a similar season again, it would be unbelievable!"

TREVOR SINCLAIR   **QUEENS PARK RANGERS**

it's quiz time!

1 Which two Scottish clubs did Gordon Strachan play for?

2 Which manager went from Sporting Lisbon to Porto?

3 If you were watching Honved play Ferencvaros, which country would you be in?

4 Who won the F.A. Cup in 1990?

5 Which Scottish club plays at Boghead Park?

6 For which Italian club did Ray Wilkins and Mark Hateley play?

7 True or false — Blackburn's Kevin Gallacher broke his leg in a league match against Spurs last season.

8 Which player holds the record for most goals scored in F.A. Cup Finals?

9 Four Englishmen have won over 100 caps. Name them.

10 Who are the current holders of the European Championships and who did they beat in the Final?

11 Who captained England in their first match under Terry Venables?

12 Who were the only team to beat Manchester United twice in the League last season?

13 Who were the beaten semi-finalists in last season's Coca Cola cup?

14 Who was top scorer in the 1990 World Cup Finals?

15 They play their matches at the Belle Vue Ground. Who are they?

16 The father of Spurs keeper Ian Walker is manager of which Premier side?

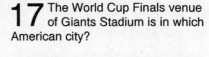
● See question 16.

17 The World Cup Finals venue of Giants Stadium is in which American city?

18 From which club did Manchester United sign Peter Schmeichel? Brondby, Lyngby or Silkeborg?

19 Who is the manager of Dundee United?

20 Who is Arsenal's most-capped player?

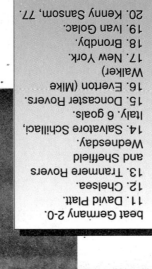
● See question 7.

LIFE BEGIN

Brian Grieves needed a challenge — and he found it!

A full-time art teacher with three grown-up kids, 40-year-old Brian felt that this was the time to start something new. So he set up his one-man operation called CLASSIC IMAGES, specialising in football sculpture. Newcastle-born Brian spends hours researching character references and still photographs of potential action subjects.

But that's only a fraction of the time he spends creating the actual sculptures!

Brian's currently working on the move leading up to Holland's penalty in the 1974 World Cup Final. It isn't finished yet, but it's bound to be another Classic!

● Figures are moulded in a very strong plaster/resin putty. Once set, this can be filed, chipped or rubbed down to suit.

● Once Brian is satisfied that every little detail is exact, the models are sent to Birmingham for bronze casting. Then, they are either painted or left in their original bronze.

Pictured here are two variations of Diego Maradona.

BEFORE

AFTER

● Here, Brian puts the finishing touches to an action image of Pele.

● The late Sir Matt Busby — commissioned by Barclays Bank on the occasion of Sir Matt's 80th Birthday.

● World Cup Finals are a strong feature of Brian's work —

England v. Holland, World Cup 1990.
England wall at free-kick. World Cup Final 1966.

GYM FIXED

SAYS **MIKE HOOPER**, NEWCASTLE

When I joined Newcastle United in September last year I knew I was in for a few surprises because the goalkeeping coach, John "Budgie" Burridge, had a reputation for doing things out of the ordinary.

So the alarm bells started to ring when John said he was taking me to a gym to do some work on developing the upper half of my body. He explained that he was also looking for ways to improve my speed and sharpness.

We pulled up at this place outside Durham and walked in. I didn't know what to expect.

I thought I was auditioning for a Rocky film. The gym was full of burly boxers and you certainly wouldn't argue with any of them.

The first time I went, I'd played just one game for Newcastle so they probably didn't know who I was, although they recognised John.

They thought I was some heavyweight who'd turned up for training. I bet someone was saying, 'He's not that badly marked, he must have good feet.'

That would be until they saw me trying to skip. Heaven knows what they thought when they saw me hitting the punch-bag!

We went once a week for the boxing work and once a week to do other gym work. He worked me hard, but I couldn't really complain because he did most of it himself!

The first time I went I was a bit miffed because I didn't know what I was getting myself into. It was also 7 p.m. on a Monday and I was going to miss Coronation Street!

He said we'd do half-an-hour's work. It turned out to be an hour and I was shattered at the end.

I wore gloves and threw punches at a punch-bag. I also did a lot of work with a medicine ball. I had to constantly keep my hands up at the level of my shoulders.

We did three-minute rounds hitting the bag. It's good for footwork and body strength in my arms and chest.

That's heavy going wearing

● JOHN BURRIDGE

gloves. Budgie was a real slave driver. But I didn't put the gloves on and hit him. We might have ended up knocking lumps out of each other!

At Liverpool I'd gone a bit flabby, but I lost a stone in the first month I was visiting the gym. Certainly, playing first-team football had a lot to do with that, but the gym work helped.

I feel my feet have become quicker because I'm required to dance around the ring to improve

my sharpness. I'm also more alert.

I'm having no alcohol, no take-away food and no late meals. At Anfield, I let things go a bit because I wasn't in the team. I hit the wall and I had no target.

There's no way I would have been taken to the gym for boxing lessons while I was at Liverpool.

I was in a catch-22 situation there before David James joined Bruce Grobbelaar and myself at the club in the summer of 1992.

The boss at the time, Graeme Souness, was scared of 'keepers being injured, so they didn't train us very hard. If something happened to Bruce, I didn't do the training.

They worked on the principle that if Bruce was injured they couldn't afford to let me take any shooting or handling practice in case I bent my finger back or suffered some other injury.

If both Bruce and myself were fit, we'd do a little bit more training, but nothing like we do at Newcastle, where you are worked into the ground regardless.

Liverpool were entitled to adopt that policy of safeguarding against injuries, but I prefer the situation at Newcastle where I have a full work-out and don't bother too much about picking up injuries.

Don't get me wrong, I really enjoyed my eight seasons at Anfield, even though I played less than 100 first-team games — well below what I would have hoped for having spent so long at the club.

During my time at Liverpool I was very loyal to them. I think people were surprised I stayed so long. But I had some good times there.

I've been to Wembley six or seven times, although I've not

IT FOR ME!

UNITED.

played there often. I did make my debut in front of a capacity crowd at Wembley in the Charity Shield. Not many players can claim that.

Goalies peak at about 30, so I don't think I had my best years at Liverpool. At 29, I still have a couple of years' improvement before I peak and then three or four years of good work.

The prospect of first-team football at Newcastle was just the opportunity I'd been looking for.

There were three goalkeepers at Liverpool and it was impossible to string together a consistent season. You knew somewhere along the line something would go wrong and you'd be out.

When I first joined Liverpool I wanted to be the club's first-choice 'keeper. But I became more philosophical about things as I grew a little older and realised that it wasn't going to happen.

You need to be of a special mental breed to play for Liverpool. Bruce has it and I thought I had it, too.

One good thing to come out of my time there was that I learned a lot from Bruce. From dealing with crosses to dealing with life in general, he has been a very good friend. I wouldn't swap the eight years with Bruce for anything.

All the three 'keepers got on well with each other. It was down to the manager who was chosen to play and we accepted that.

I left Anfield with no ill-feelings and wish Liverpool all the best for the future. But my future lies elsewhere at Newcastle and I look on it as a new beginning.

Newcastle have shown faith in me by offering me a contract at St James' Park and giving me a long run in the first-team. I hope I can repay them for the boost they've given my career.

marathon man

THIS IS THE LONG-TERM AMBITION OF QUEENS PARK RANGERS' LES FERDINAND...

EVERY footballer has the usual ambitions — playing for their country, winning the FA Cup and so on.

But I have an added target outside of football.

I want to run in the London Marathon.

The timing of the race, in April, makes that impossible while I am still playing professional football. QPR wouldn't be too happy if I turned up for training with blistered feet and heavy legs, after running 26 miles, 385 yards!

But when I finally pack up playing football for a living, my aim will be to complete the marathon.

The incentive for me is to raise money for the Imperial Cancer Research charity. I have been involved with the charity for a couple of years now.

My mum died from cancer four years ago. We were so close, I felt I had to do something in her memory.

My dad left home when I was eight years old. My mum had to be like a father and a mother to me.

There's never been a day since she died that I haven't thought about her.

It was a great disappointment to me that she never lived to see me play for England. Mum would have been very proud to see me wearing an England shirt.

Once I had won my first cap, I felt I could use my name to help raise money for cancer charities.

I wrote to Imperial Cancer Research to offer my help. My idea was to ask any football fans entered for the London Marathon to run for the charity.

I wrote to all the football clubs asking them to pass on my request in their club pro-

gramme. Also, I wrote a press release to send to some local papers.

The response was encouraging. About 40 runners responded to the appeal and raised several thousand pounds for the charity. It was very rewarding.

Last summer I also got involved in the Corporate Games — a multi-sports event for company teams — at Milton Keynes. Their nominated charity was Imperial Cancer Research.

I'm very happy to give my time. It was a great thrill to think that people were running the marathon to raise money on my behalf.

I'd like to run in the race myself, but that will have to wait. But at least I feel I'm doing something by getting involved.

My mum did everything for me. By helping to raise money for charity, I can at least help other cancer victims.

Last season was a frustrating one, at club and international level. Failing to qualify for the World Cup finals was a big disappointment.

At QPR we felt we were good enough to gain a UEFA Cup place, but in the end we missed out. And we had a bad defeat in the FA Cup at Stockport.

This season I would like to think I can win a medal in one of the competitions. That's my football ambition.

While my mum did so much for me early in life, it's my QPR boss Gerry Francis and former team-mate Ray Wilkins who have helped me establish myself in the last couple of years.

They gave me the confidence and determination to work at my game.

Gerry told me early on that I had the ability to play for England if I believed in myself and worked hard. It's great to play for a manager who has faith in you.

In the past, I used to lose

confidence quickly, especially if I wasn't scoring goals. Gerry and Ray were always on at me to keep going.

As a youngster I was always a bit laid-back. I would take the easy option.

They showed me what I could do if I knuckled down and worked at my game. My first England cap was as much due to them as to me.

Once I had a taste of international football I wanted to stay on the scene. I think I have the natural pace and strength to hold my own at that level.

Gerry Francis has helped me in another way. When I had back trouble a couple of years ago, he put me in touch with the man who saved his own playing career.

The manager had a terrible back problem at the time when he was captain of England. It ended his international career and nearly prevented him playing again.

Gerry went to a lot of specialists, but none could help him. He was on the point of giving up the game when somebody recommended an osteopath, named Terry Moule.

He took one look at Gerry's back and told him he would be playing again within three weeks — and if he wasn't he wouldn't have to pay a penny for his treatment.

Terry Moule did the trick for Gerry. He was able to play on for several more years.

As soon as I developed a back problem, Gerry sent me to his osteopath. I have a bulging disc, which produces pain in my hamstring.

Every time I feel it, I go to Terry for manipulation and he can keep me playing. The injury is under control, although one day I may need surgery.

When people do a lot for you, it makes you want to give something back in return. That's why I'm so happy to give time to Imperial Cancer Research.

● London marathon, 19??. Les could be somewhere in there one day!

The PERFECT PARTNERSHIP

First Division Clanville Rovers were among the contenders for promotion because of their prolific strike-force, veteran thirty-year-old Gavin Bishop and nineteen-year-old Craig Manley. The combination was responsible for most of Rovers' goals, but Gavin took all the credit . . .

INCH-PERFECT! GO ON, BISH . . . BURY IT!

LOVELY BALL BY MANLEY!

GO-A-A-L!

I COULD HAVE PLACED IT, BUT THE CROWD LOVE A POWERHOUSE FINISH!

In the second-half —

YOURS, SON. GO YOURSELF!

GO, SON, GO. ALL THE WAY!

KEEP GOING, SON! THERE'S NO-ONE ELSE UP WITH YOU!

OH, BRILLIANT STUFF! HE'S WALTZED THROUGH THE LOT OF 'EM!

WHAT A FINISH! GOAL OF THE SEASON, THAT WAS!

SUPER GOAL, SON. THAT'S YOUR BEST EVER!

MAGIC, MANNERS!

NICE ONE, SON! KEEP FEEDING OFF ME AND YOU'LL DO OKAY!

CHEEKY SO-AND-SO! ALL HE DID WAS GIVE ME A TEN-YARD PASS. I DID THE REST!

After the match, with manager Graham Neill —

WONDERFUL GOAL, CRAIG. WELL DONE!

NOT BAD. ONE DAY HE'LL BE AS GOOD AS ME, BOSS!

The youngster was used to Bishop's comments and ignored them. At training the following Tuesday —

WOW! EVEN MARK HUGHES WOULD HAVE BEEN PROUD OF THAT ONE!

FULL MARKS FOR TECHNICAL MERIT AND ARTISTIC ABILITY!

HERE, LET ME HELP YOU UP, WONDER-BOY!

OH, LEAVE IT OUT, LADS . . .

When Rovers players arrived for their next home game —

HEY, LADS . . . SEEN WHO'S HERE TODAY? THE CHIDSEA SCOUT, BOB FERRIS!

IT'LL BE ME HE'S WATCHING! MAKE SURE YOU TEE A FEW UP FOR ME, SON!

NOW, KID . . . NEAR POST!

GREAT FINISH! THAT'LL IMPRESS FERRIS!

WHAT A GOAL!

YEE-SS!

Bishop wanted the ball at every opportunity —

TWO-NIL! BISHOP AGAIN!

SET UP BY YOUNG MANLEY — AGAIN!

YEE-SS! DID YOU SEE THAT ONE, FERRIS?

But it was Craig who provided the afternoon's outstanding moment —

LOOK AT THE KID GO!

THE BALL'S GLUED TO HIS FEET!

PENALTY! STONE-WALLER, TOO!

IT'S NOT FAIR! I DO ALL THE WORK — HE GRABS THE GLORY!

I'LL TAKE IT, SON. I'M ON A HAT-TRICK, REMEMBER!

GAVIN BISHOP! THREE-NIL!

EASY! EASY!

THAT SHOULD HAVE SEALED IT. PREMIER LEAGUE HERE I COME!

When Craig arrived at the ground on Monday morning —

MORNING, CRAIG. THE BOSS WANTS TO SEE YOU BEFORE TRAINING.

THANKS, JULIE.

. . . SO THAT'S IT, SON . . . CHIDSEA HAVE MADE THEIR BID. WE'D LOVE TO KEEP YOU, BUT WE CAN'T TURN DOWN A MILLION QUID!

I-I'M GOBSMACKED, BOSS! I THOUGHT THEY'D COME IN FOR GAVIN . . .

Gavin was equally surprised when he heard the news —

WHAAAT? YOU'RE WINDING ME UP!

IT'S TRUE, GAV. CRAIG'S AWAY TO CHIDSEA — FOR ONE MILLION!

Craig's new striking partner, Terry James, was waiting to greet him on his arrival —

THOUGHT I'D BETTER COME AND MEET YOU AS WE'RE TO BE PARTNERING EACH OTHER UP FRONT FOR THE REST OF THE SEASON.

THAT'S VERY NICE OF YOU, TERRY. GOOD TO MEET YOU, TOO!

The two immediately hit it off —

GREAT STRIKE, MANNERS!

BRILLIANT MOVE, LADS. DO THAT ON SATURDAY AND WE'LL BE FLYING!

There was a capacity crowd for Craig's debut in the derby match against Tottenford —

ONE CRAIG MANLEY . . . THERE'S ONLY ONE CRAIG MANLEY . . .

THEY LIKE YOU, SON. AND THEY'LL LIKE YOU EVEN BETTER AFTER THIS!

The new partnership soon clicked —

WHAT A GOAL!

SENSATIONAL STUFF FROM CRAIG AND TERRY!

Then it was Terry's turn to set up Craig —

TERRY TO CRAIG! TWO-ONE!

BRILLIANT! BISHOP WOULD NEVER SET ME UP LIKE THAT!

Terry set Craig up again for the decisive third

LOVELY BALL TO YOUNG MANNERS!

HE'S IN! HIT IT, SON!

THREE-NIL! WHAT A SHOT!

Afterwards —

YOU KNOW, BOSS, WHEN I CAME HERE, I THOUGHT IT WAS TO REPLACE TERRY.

NO WAY, SON. YOU AND BISHOP WERE A GOOD PARTNERSHIP . . .

. . . BUT YOU AND TERRY WILL BE THE PERFECT PARTNERSHIP!

THE END

face-off football

By CRAIG FORREST, Ipswich Town

ICE HOCKEY is the big game in Canada where I was born. Like every other kid I wanted to pull my skates on and get out there on the rink.

I was a good, fast skater but I had to learn to take the hits like everybody else. You can't avoid getting clobbered in ice-hockey. It's a very tough game, always played close to the edge.

For ten years I played ice-hockey to a good standard. Some of my team-mates were signed up to play in the National Hockey League.

I could have got close to the top myself but I had my eyes on playing a different kind of sport — football. To do that I had to travel to England where I joined Ipswich Town.

I hadn't played as a goal-minder in ice-hockey, I was actually a winger, but it was still good preparation for being a goalkeeper in football. You get plenty of knocks from big centre-forwards in the English game.

Football is popular in Canada but unfortunately the game hasn't been very well organised over the years. I think most of the people that got involved in the game were far more interested in American Football, basketball and ice-hockey.

I don't think they had the best interests of football at heart. It started off well but turned out to be a Mickey Mouse league in the end.

The big-time for football in Canada came in the late 1970's and 1980's. A lot of good players played for my local club, Vancouver Whitecaps, during that period.

Peter Beardsley and Bruce Grobbelaar were there at the start of their careers and players like Trevor Whymark, Frans Thijssen and Kevin Hector all ended up there at the end of their playing days.

With Whymark and Thijssen having played for Ipswich, it's perhaps not surprising I ended up at Portman Road as an apprentice. I knew it was a good place to learn the

⬤ Canadian Ice Hockey has done all right without Craig Forrest. The Canadian national team reached the finals of the Winter Olympics in Lillehammer last February.

game properly.

People in Canada are still following my fortunes in the game. I still get letters from there, expecially when I've been home to play for the national team. They like to wish me all the best.

In the run-up to the World Cup it all got very exciting. We did well in our qualifying group but just missed out in a play-off with Australia. They were then knocked out themselves by Argentina in a final eliminator for the World Cup Finals.

Our compensation was that we still got to play some of the top teams in the world like Germany and Holland, who were looking for friendlies before the World Cup itself.

The English game gets good coverage on Canadian TV's Soccer Saturday Show but that doesn't mean I'm asked to do interviews all the time. They like to give neutral coverage with no special treatment for myself or fellow Canadian Paul Peschisolido.

The game has really picked up in Canada. With the World Cup having been played in the United States this year, lots of people have been watching the game on the TV.

I have to admit that before we did so well in the World Cup qualifiers, I was far more interested in playing for Ipswich Town. They paid my wages and playing international

injuries. Ice-hockey players get a lot of hernias and stomach problems, so there are plenty of specialists in that area.

North American sports stars take an awful battering during their careers. I was lucky to escape serious injury playing ice-hockey myself, but a lot of the top players in that sport and American Football end up in a terrible state. Some of the knee injuries can be horrific.

We're very lucky at Ipswich because our own physio has learned from attending seminars in America. He's helped to build up one of the best treatment centres in England by studying how Americans treat injuries.

I can now feel confident about getting the best possible treatment if I get injured myself.

Thankfully I recovered from my stomach problems to have a good run of form for Ipswich last season. It was a better year for the team as well.

The year before, I'd had to watch from the sidelines as they slipped further and further towards the relegation zone.

But last season we tightened up a lot at the back. Some people called us boring, but we knew that our priority had to be to stay in the Premier League.

matches put my first-team place in jeopardy.

It wasn't just me at the time either. Ipswich team-mate Frank Yallop was also called up for the national team.

It didn't help matters when I picked up a bad injury when I was on international duty. I missed over half a season because of that, which was very annoying.

The problem was badly ruptured stomach muscles, but I kept getting different opinions on the problem from both sides of the Atlantic. Nobody seemed to know exactly what was wrong.

One expert would tell me to go out and play, the next would say rest. I was very worried about it for a time and didn't know if it would ever get better.

The good thing about having contacts in North America is that they are very advanced in their treatment of sports

JOHN SCALES had to admit he'd been wrong. Playing for Wimbledon didn't stop you getting called up for international duty.

England coach Terry Venables finally gave Scales the recognition he deserved at the end of last season.

For years Scales has been rated one of the country's top centre-backs. Cool under pressure, he has consistently kept the country's top strikers quiet with his quality performances at the heart of the Dons' defence.

But playing for a so-called 'unfashionable' club was thought to have cost him his England chance during Graham Taylor's time as England manager.

Then, just when he was beginning to wonder whether he would ever play for his country, Venables picked Scales in an England B team against Northern Ireland.

It didn't end there either. Having scored a rare goal in the B match, he was immediately put on stand-by for the full squad. The season ended with Scales on the bench for the game against Norway.

"That all proved that Terry Venables was prepared to pick players from the so-called smaller clubs," says John.

"Just a week before the Norway game I'd been at Wembley watching my mate Dennis Wise play for Chelsea in the FA Cup Final. I had no idea that I'd be sitting on the bench for England so soon after.

"Warren Barton was also in that England squad with me, and Dean Holdsworth played and scored for the England B team against Northern Ireland.

"We hadn't been very lucky at Wimbledon with England recognition over the years. There were several players who might have been picked at one stage or another.

"I was as ambitious as anybody to play for my country. Like the rest of the lads, I knew I just had to keep playing to the best of my ability.

"When the recognition finally came it was no more than the whole team deserved last season. We proved we had the quality to compete with the very best.

"There's nothing the Wimbledon lads like more than beating the big boys. And we did plenty of that last season including claiming the scalps of the Premiership's top three Manchester United, Blackburn Rovers and Newcastle United.

"The quality of teams like that show how much the top league has improved in recent years — and Wimbledon have improved too.

"Besides beating the big boys, we also made quite an impact on the relegation battle by beating several of the struggling teams. Wimbledon just love making an impact.

"By the end of last season I knew I was playing in the best Wimbledon team since I joined the club from Bristol Rovers seven years ago. It compared very favourably with the team that had won the 1988 FA Cup Final against Liverpool.

"One of the big differences was that we had a regular goalscorer in Dean Holdsworth. Every top team needs a player capable of scoring over 20 goals a season and Deano fits the bill.

"But much of the credit for last season has to go to manager Joe Kinnear. He had a terrific year, scooping three 'Manager of the month' awards.

"That was no fluke. He had the team playing some good football last season and deserved everything he received."

Wimbledon's unlikely success story has inevitably brought envious advances from other clubs over the years. Every year Scales found himself the subject of big-money transfer speculation.

"It's always been a fact of life at Wimbledon," says Scales. "You just had to accept it and get on with playing.

"All the interest is just taken as a compliment by the club. It's good for Wimbledon to have such highly-rated players.

"I never let it bother me personally. Of course I was aware of any interest but it didn't unsettle me.

"The fact is that everybody loves playing for Wimbledon so much that nobody is ever that desperate to leave. The atmosphere and team spirit at the club is wonderful.

"That's what has always made Wimbledon such dangerous opponents. The team has never needed any extra incentive to win matches.

"Whether up against a championship-chasing team or one trying to avoid relegation, Wimbledon are always the team nobody wants to play."

WIMBLEDON'S JOHN SCALES COULDN'T HAVE HAD A BETTER ENDING TO LAST SEASON!

dream topping!

HENNING BERG

BLACKBURN ROVERS

IAN WRIGHT   **ARSENAL**

● Ready and waiting, all eyes on the ball. A Liverpool defensive wall - plus Sheffield Wednesday's Ryan Jones.

● Time to take evasive action...

●...as Wednesday's Chris Waddle fires in a free-kick!

firing squad

King of the Kop

The story of Kenny Dalglish

Kenny Dalglish... the football genius whose talents won him honours galore with Celtic and Liverpool. This is the story of how a football-mad youngster became one of the finest players ever to grace British soccer.

Although he was to win fame and fortune with Celtic, it was their fierce rivals, Rangers, Dalglish supported as a boy.

With encouragement from his father, Dalglish progressed from Glasgow Schoolboys to Scotland Schoolboys, making his international debut in May 1966 in Belfast. Scotland won 4-3 with Kenny scoring a couple of goals.

When Glasgow Celtic swooped for Kenny in May 1967, Kenny tore down all the photographs of his Rangers idols like Jim Baxter.

Dalglish made his first-team debut for the Parkhead side on 25th September 1968 and that was the start of a Celtic career which saw him win five Championships, four Scottish Cups and one League Cup, scoring over 150 goals in the process.

The first of 102 Scotland caps — a record — was won in November 1971. He also scored 30 goals for his country, equalling the record of Denis Law.

Dalglish's 100th cap was recognised by a silver and gold "cap" presented by Franz Beckenbauer.

After an illustrious career with Celtic, Dalglish moved south to Liverpool for a then record fee of £440,000 in 1977. He was soon amongst the silverware there, netting the winner in the 1978 European Cup Final v. Bruges.

Dalglish's services to football were rewarded with an MBE in 1984.

In 1985, Dalglish was appointed player/manager of Liverpool, and in the following season the Anfield side won the double — the first ever by a player/manager. Dalglish's goal against Chelsea at Stamford Bridge was the Championship clincher.

With Liverpool, he continued where he had left off with Celtic. Five Championships, four League Cups and three European Cups were won. He scored over 150 goals — the only man to do so north and south of the border.

As player/manager, he won three Championships and two F.A. Cups.

Then — sensation! The football world was stunned when Dalglish tendered his resignation in Feburary 1991. Had the pressure of keeping Liverpool at the top got to him?

With big-money buys like goal-happy Alan Shearer, Dalglish has fashioned Blackburn into a potent force. So far, the silverware has eluded him at Ewood Park, but will it only be a matter of time . . . ?

But Kenny couldn't last long out of football and was tempted to big-money Blackburn in October of that year. Soon, he was back at a happy hunting ground of his — Wembley — steering the Second Division club to victory in the play-offs. Dalglish was back!

SITTING on the touch-line in Copenhagen, watching Arsenal play in the European Cup Winners Cup final, was the biggest disappointment of my life.

When I helped my team reach the final, by beating Paris St Germain at Highbury, it was one of the highlights of my career. For the first time I really felt I was appreciated by the fans on the terraces.

Winning the semi-final meant I would be playing against Parma in the final, in my home town of Copenhagen. All my family would be there to see me.

It was a wonderful feeling. But a week later I was brought down to earth — by a sad coincidence in Copenhagen.

Playing for Denmark, in a friendly international against Hungary, I was injured by a very bad tackle that ended my hopes of playing in the Cup Winners Cup.

I couldn't believe it. Things had been going so well for me.

Now I have to hope that we have another chance to win a medal in European competition.

The Cup Winners Cup matches were very good for me last season. They helped me to establish myself in the eyes of the fans.

My first season at Highbury was a bit of a struggle. I arrived very tired after helping Denmark win the European Championship, and went into the season without a proper break.

It was very hard work. In mid-season I had to take a rest, and then it was hard to regain my place in the team.

I missed the Coca-Cola Cup Final, but managed to earn a place in the FA Cup Finals.

One problem was that the fans expected something different from me. They saw me scoring a spectacular goal in the European Championships Final against Germany, and thought I would do the same at Highbury.

But that's not really my game. I've never been an attacking midfield player.

My strengths have always been as an anchor man, winning the ball and moving it on quickly to a more creative player. In my professional career, I've never scored more than three or four goals in a season.

But when I came to Arsenal, I think people wanted to see me scoring great goals. The fans didn't realise that George Graham had signed me for my other qualities.

The Cup Winners Cup games, particularly the quarter-finals against Torino, and the semis against Paris St Germain, were ideal for me to show my real strengths.

goal drou

I feel I'm now accepted by the fans for what I am — the 'holding' man in midfield. The role doesn't give me much chance to get forward.

There has to be a balance in the side. We can't all be attacking players.

The supporters now realise that. In my first year they wanted me to score goals. I wanted to score goals too, but we are all still waiting!

People have said that my European Championship goal was a millstone round my neck. I never believed it — I enjoyed it too much to ever think that.

The supporters last season made me a hero for not scoring goals. I didn't mind.

To me, English fans are the best in the world. They are much more part of the game than in Denmark or Germany.

I love to hear the fans singing. There are more football songs in England than anywhere else in the world.

And the best thing is that English fans never stop singing. In other countries they sing and shout, but only when a goal is scored.

Here they sing for anything. You can chase for an impossible ball, and fail to catch it, but the crowd will chant your name because you made the effort.

That means a lot to any player. It really lifts you to hear the fans sing your name.

Reaching the Cup Winners Cup final helped to make up for the disappointment of Denmark failing to qualify for the World Cup finals. Like England, we fell at the last hurdle.

That was a huge blow to me. After the European success, I felt we would do really well in the USA.

We felt we could have reached at least the quarter-finals of the World Cup. I believe we were a better team than either Spain or Ireland, who did qualify from our group.

But that's the way football is. Full of ups and downs. Now Denmark have to make a good job of defending our European title.

The first task is to qualify for the finals, which are being held in England. We hope to get our revenge against Spain and Belgium who will also be tough opponents.

I desperately want to play in the finals in 1996. Being so settled here, it will be almost like playing at home for me.

It would help make up for missing my other 'home' game in Copenhagen last season.

John celebrates his glory goal in the 1992 European Championships v. Germany.

ght

. . . BUT ARSENAL'S JOHN JENSEN DOESN'T MIND!

better late than never!

KEVIN RICHARDSON
ASTON VILLA

AN England debut at the age of 31 . . . a League Cup Final win at the third attempt . . . the start of another European campaign. It has all been happening for Aston Villa skipper Kevin Richardson during the past few months.

And despite approaching an age associated with a waning career, the battling midfielder is determined to prove that his years will be no barrier to future success.

Richardson, who won League Championship medals in his 20s with Everton and Arsenal and still aims to be the first player to attain a trio of titles with three different clubs, is currently enjoying his second wave of success in England.

There are many who believe that his international recognition — he made his full England debut in the 5-0 Wembley victory over Greece last May — was long overdue.

For three years, since manager Ron Atkinson signed him from Spanish club Real Sociedad, he has been the unsung hero of the Villa side. The midfield grafter who quietly gets on with his job, battling 100 per cent for 90 minutes, but sometimes goes unnoticed because there is nothing fancy about the way he plays.

But Richardson will be happy to carry on that way if it means staying at the top for another half a decade.

He explains, "Though I am 31, I believe I can play at this level until I am well into my 30s, just as Gordon Strachan, Ray Wilkins and Bryan Robson have done.

"All three are an example to every player in the League. They have shown that, by looking after yourself properly, you can remain in the game for a long time.

"I have always made a point of looking after my body properly, so there is no reason why I can't prove the point myself.

"Working hard in training is vital, of course, but it is only part of the process. Your diet is equally important.

"At Villa, we have regular visits from experts

who explain what we should be eating, and I always read the dieticians' columns in the magazines. I stick rigidly to a diet which contains a lot of fish, chicken and pasta, ensuring that I get a lot of protein and carbohydrates."

Ironically, the key to much of Richardson's recent success with Villa came as a result of a penalty shoot-out in which he missed a vital penalty, the memory of which still haunts him.

The drama unfolded at the climax of their Coca-Cola Cup semi-final second leg against Tranmere Rovers at Villa Park.

Ron Atkinson's side appeared to be on their way out of the competition until a last-gasp equaliser by Dalian Atkinson threw them a lifeline — and led eventually to the shoot-out.

After the first phase of five spot-kicks by each side the scores were level, so it became a matter of sudden death.

With no volunteers to take the vital next penalty, Richardson shouldered the responsibility, and set the Villa fans squirming.

His previous penalty attempt had been in an FA Cup shoot-out against Wimbledon a season earlier, and he fired the ball over the crossbar to send his side out of the tournament.

To Kevin's horror, he repeated the miss, and Tranmere's Liam O'Brien was presented with a chance to shoot his side into the final.

Kevin is still embarrassed as he recalls the moment. He says, "The picture of my miss will stay with me for a very long time. If we had gone out, I would never have stopped blaming myself.

"We had not agreed on an order of penalty-takers if the shoot-out went into sudden death. When it did reach that stage, I asked the lads, 'Who wants to take it?'

"Nobody spoke up, so there was nothing else for it. I made a captain's decision, and went up to take the kick myself.

"As I walked towards the penalty spot, there must have been plenty of Villa fans remembering my effort against Wimbledon and thinking, 'Oh no, not Richardson!'

"But the thought of that miss did not occur to me. I was simply making up my mind about how I was going to deliver this one. I decided that I was going to blast it and carried a picture in my head of the ball hitting the net.

"Unfortunately, I got underneath it and leaned back too much, which made me knock it into the second tier of the executive boxes!

"I felt empty. I was completely numb as I walked back to the centre circle, then I felt the pressure build up inside me as I watched the remainder of the shoot-out. I can't tell you how grateful I was to our goalkeeper, Mark Bosnich, when he got me out of a dodgy situation by saving O'Brien's penalty.

"Then, when Bossie made the winning save from Ian Nolan, I just took off. It all came out of me at once, and I was running about the pitch like a hooligan, more through relief than anything else."

Villa were in the final, and Richardson had a chance to lay his hands on a trophy which he had come so close to winning twice before. But on each occasion, while playing for Everton in 1984 and Arsenal in 1988, he had to be content with a runners-up medal.

This time, however, he made it third time lucky as Villa upset the odds by outplaying Manchester United at Wembley and running

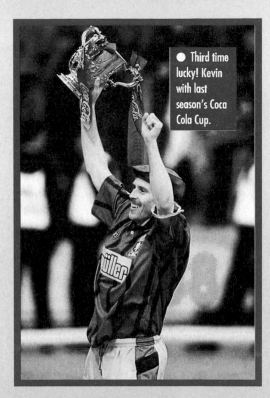

● Third time lucky! Kevin with last season's Coca Cola Cup.

out deserved 3-1 winners.

It was his first trophy as a Villa player. But Kevin reveals that, when he joined the club back in 1991, his main aim was simply to prove that he was still capable of playing regular top-flight football.

He goes on, "I will always be grateful to the club for giving me the chance of stepping straight back into top-flight football when I returned from Spain.

"Though I had never lost faith in my ability, there was always a doubt in my mind that I would be given such a chance.

"When you go abroad, you can easily be forgotten, unless you are playing in the high-profile Italian League or for one of the top Spanish clubs — Real Madrid or Barcelona.

"Real Sociedad were a middle-of-the-road, improving club. Though I was very grateful to them for giving me the opportunity of seeing the other side of football's coin, they probably meant nothing to people back home in England, so I'm sure I became a back number.

"I would have liked to have stayed there for longer than just a year, but my return was not my decision. It resulted from the manager being sacked, which is a common occurence in Spain.

"When his successor arrived, he introduced different ideas and made it clear that I would be leaving in the summer.

"Having been at big clubs before I left England in the first place, I felt sure that people in the game would know what I could do and hoped they hadn't forgotten that. In the end, I'm sure it was my old Everton teammate, Andy Gray, who helped me return to a top English club.

"He was the assistant manager at Villa then, and I think he must have put a good word in for me.

"I came here feeling that I had to prove myself all over again since my departure from the English game. Fortunately, things have worked out pretty well during the past three years."

DES WALKER　　　　　　　　　**SHEFFIELD WEDNESDAY**

DARREN ANDERTON   **SPURS**

A
TALE
OF
TWO
PENALTIES
IN THE
CAREER OF
SWINDON'S
**PAUL
BODIN**

a hit and

PAUL BODIN will always be remembered as the player who missed the penalty that could have taken Wales to the World Cup Finals.

It was a night full of tension at Cardiff Arms Park. An excited crowd knew that a win over Romania would take their heroes to the USA.

The game was finely poised at 1-1 after 62 minutes when Wales dramatically got the break they needed. Gary Speed was pulled down in the box and the referee immediately pointed to the spot.

Up stepped Bodin with the whole of Wales behind him. He struck the ball hard but the Wales players could only hang their heads in disbelief as it crashed against the bar and rebounded away.

It was over for Wales. Romania went on to win the match and themselves qualify for the Finals.

Paul Bodin was left to have nightmares about that fatal

● Paul's fateful penalty kick v. Romania.

miss. But it didn't put him off taking another when the chance came.

"I went through that penalty time and time again in my mind," says Paul. "But Swindon boss John Gorman told me to forget all about it and to remember that I was still the club's number one penalty taker.

"Thankfully, I got a chance to take another one very quickly. As usual I hit it high and hard and this time it hit the back of the net.

"Even when I missed one later on, people at the club were quick to remind me that at least I'd given the club the chance to play in the Premiership in the first place.

"I scored the penalty that finally beat Leicester City in the 1993 Division One Play-Off Final. In a very exciting match, Leicester had come back at us from 3-0 down to level at 3-3.

"Then, with just six minutes left, we were given a penalty. I stepped forward, scored and we were on our way into the Premier League.

"That was a very emotional experience for me. I was a bit nervous before I took the kick but I struck it well, the 'keeper committed himself and it went in. It really is a great feeling when you see the ball hit the back of the net.

"I got the chance to take penalties at several more big grounds last season, including Manchester United, Tottenham and Arsenal. Thankfully I scored at all three.

"But Arsenal's Ian Wright didn't miss the chance to remind me about my miss in the World Cup game. He was trying to put me off, of course, but I just hit it the same as ever and I managed to beat David Seaman."

The World Cup defeat was to cost Welsh manager Terry Yorath his job. John Toshack was brought in as his replacement and what turned out to be his one and only squad didn't include the unfortunate Paul Bodin.

"I missed out on a whole regime when John Toshack left me out," says Paul. "A few weeks after the team had lost to Norway, he resigned and Mike Smith took over. Then I was back in again.

"It wasn't an easy season for me to make an impression because we had such a hard campaign at Swindon. We had to learn a lot of very harsh lessons in the Premiership.

"Basically we were caught out by the clinical nature of the game at the highest level. Quality strikers made us pay heavily for our mistakes.

"At the other end of the pitch we didn't have the killer touch ourselves. We showed we were capable of playing some great football but we just couldn't finish opponents off in games.

"We'd had just one short season in the Premiership. It had been quite an experience."

MOWLEM

a miss

GOALKEEPER Ludek Miklosko played a major role in helping West Ham establish a place in the Premier League last season.

But it took a brave decision from Miklosko to allow him to concentrate on his career with the Hammers.

At the age of 32 — a stage at which many goalkeepers are just reaching their prime — Ludek turned his back on international football with the Czech Republic.

Miklosko informed the Czech team boss that he didn't wish to be considered any further for national team selection. It meant the tall 'keeper was able to put all his attention and energy into his club performances.

Ludo is desperate to win honours at club level. He doesn't want the distraction of international call-ups — and the possibility of missing vital club matches — to interfere with his ambitions.

But it still took some soul-searching before he took the decision.

"My future is with West Ham United. I decided to tell the Czech officials not to pick me any more," says Miklosko.

"I loved playing for my country. Every footballer enjoys international football.

"But I came to the decision that I

didn't want to carry on any longer. I felt it wasn't fair to anybody if I continued to play for the Czech Republic.

"If I had to go off to play all the Czech international matches, that wouldn't be fair to West Ham. The club pay my wages, but I would miss important games.

"If I were to play just some international games, like European Championship matches, that wouldn't be fair to the other Czech goalkeepers.

"I don't want that. I'm very happy in England, and I want to concentrate on playing for West Ham.

"There are some good young 'keepers coming through for the Czechs. They have to be given the chance to play international football and gain experience.

"My career is at Upton Park. It's my ambition to win some medals with West Ham.

"Maybe I'm not an Englishman. But after more than four years here, I am a little bit like one."

Miklosko has had an up-and-down time at West Ham. He joined the club in the Second Division and has been promoted twice and relegated once.

His own form has generally been more consistent than the team's performance, but he plays down his part.

"It's a team game. We defend as a team, it's not just one player," says Ludo.

"A goalkeeper needs some luck. It's not possible to play perfectly in every game of the season.

"I have made some mistakes, and when a goalkeeper makes an error it usually means a goal. Everybody has a bad game sometimes.

"But we worked very hard last season. There was a very good atmosphere in the club. Everyone was working for the team."

After nearly five years, Miklosko is very much part of the East London scene. His wife Ivana and thirteen-year-old son Martin are happily settled in Essex.

But they arrived from Ostrava without a word of English between them and the early days were not easy.

"I came to England without knowing a word of English," admits Ludo. "I couldn't understand the people, the newspapers or the TV.

"It was hard to learn, but I expected that. I didn't underestimate the problems.

"We had private English lessons once a week. We made steady progress — but I hated doing the homework!

"Fortunately, I think it is easier for a goalkeeper than an outfield player to adjust to playing in a different country. Goalkeeping is not so different where ever you play.

"After ten years in the game, it might have been hard for me to change too much. I didn't need to.

"The only difference was that English football is much faster than the game back home. And there are many more matches.

"At home I was used to a mid-winter break as well. But I don't mind being kept busy. It's more exciting that way.

"I enjoy playing football here. I'm very settled. I hope that I can help West Ham win some trophies in the next year or two."

WEST HAM'S **LUDEK MIKLOSKO** PREFERS THE LIFE OF AN EASTENDER TO THAT OF AN INTERNA-TIONALIST.

club before country

MATTHEW LE TISSIER'S spectacular one-man show saved Southampton's Premiership skins last season — and won him a place in the England squad.

Nobody scores goals quite like the man from Guernsey. He could have had a 'Goal of the Season' competition all to himself for the 1993-94 campaign.

Mat has had a video put together of all the goals he's scored during his career — and there aren't too many tap-ins from close range. But he knows that in the last few months of the season it was quantity more than quality that counted for Southampton.

He played a magnificent captain's part in the Saints' great escape from relegation by scoring 15 of the team's last 25 goals. A player once accused of being lazy had shown just how much he cared about his team.

"The goals were flying in from all over the place last season," says Mat.

"Thankfully they didn't stop going in when it really counted towards the end of the season.

"I suppose the goal that gave me most pleasure last season would have to be the second goal I scored against Newcastle at The Dell. The ball just kept falling for me before I finally volleyed it home.

"The best strike would have to be the one against Liverpool, which came after just 27 seconds of the game. I hadn't realised it was quite so quick until I was interviewed on Sky TV after the match.

"You lose track of time when the whistle blows to start a game. I just knew it must have been early on because I wasn't tired."

Le Tissier followed up that early goal with two penalties to complete a famous hat-trick. More importantly,

Southampton beat Liverpool 4-2 to secure three valuable points.

That match came soon after Alan Ball had been appointed manager at Southampton. But it was the previous manager Ian Branfoot who had made the rather surprising decision to make Le Tissier team captain.

"It happened at Everton in December," Mat continues. "We were sitting in the dressing-room at about 2.10 p.m. when Ian Branfoot came up and said 'I want you to be captain today'.

saints

"I thought he was joking so I said 'not before time'. But he was very serious and 45 minutes later I found myself leading the team out at Goodison Park.

"The rest of the lads were just as surprised by the decision as me. I'm not sure what they thought by the end of the season.

"I just know I was chuffed to bits to be wearing the captain's armband and leading the team out for every game. And when I feel good about myself, I usually play well.

"Looking back now, that decision certainly brought the best out of me. At times I'd been accused of drifting out of games but now I had to be involved.

"At last I was playing in a position I enjoyed, and with the responsibility I needed. From that point on I was at least 20% more involved in games.

"I've never minded working hard as long as it's with the ball at my feet. I need as much of the ball as possible and thankfully my team-mates provided me with plenty last season."

The new-improved Matthew Le Tissier quickly came to the attention of England coach Terry Venables, who was on the look-out for skilful players for his team.

The new system looked perfect for Mat's game. Not surprisingly, he was mentioned as the natural replacement for the injured Paul Gascoigne.

"I'm quite happy to be compared to Gazza," says Mat. "I can handle that sort of attention.

"Playing for England has always been my main ambition in the game. If I can achieve that when playing for Southampton, I'm happy.

"Towards the end of last season, when relegation was becoming a real threat, I did wonder if I would have to move on to keep involved with England. But once we'd stayed-up, I signed a new contract to remain at The Dell.

"Southampton has been a great club for me. It's always suited me both as a player and a person.

"I think I developed considerably as a player last season. Now I want to continue that progress at both League and international level.

"People have always asked me how ambitious I am. I've always said that playing for England was the pinnacle as far as I was concerned.

"When I used to watch England, I was just like any other fan wanting them to win. Now I've been given the chance to actually help them win. No player can ask for more than that."

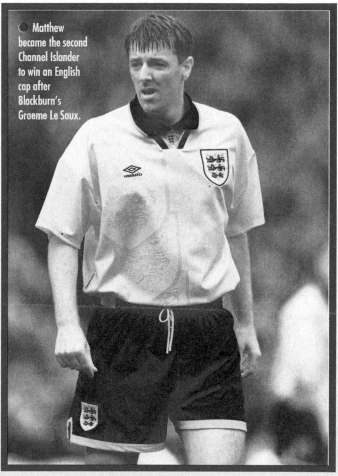

● Matthew became the second Channel Islander to win an English cap after Blackburn's Graeme Le Saux.

alive!

SOUTHAMPTON SURVIVED IN THE PREMIER LEAGUE — THANKS MAINLY TO THE GOALS OF **MATTHEW LE TISSIER**

"make the most of it!"

Says ROB NEWMAN, NORWICH CITY

ROB NEWMAN felt ten feet tall when he led Norwich City out as captain to play a UEFA Cup game against the great Inter Milan. It was a moment to savour in any player's career.

Playing at the magnificent San Siro stadium was a million miles away from the low point of his career almost exactly ten years earlier.

In December 1983, Newman was a young player in a struggling Bristol City team. In fact, after a game at Rochdale they hit rock bottom.

A 1-0 defeat at Spotland left City propping up the rest of the League as the bottom team in the old Division Four. You can't get any lower than that.

That experience has helped Newman in his career ever since. So, when he stepped out onto the San Siro pitch, he was determined to enjoy every minute.

"When you've been down to the lowest possible point in the Football League as I have, you make the most of such great occasions when they come around.

"It's not much fun being at the bottom, I can tell you, so when you get to the top level you want to stay there. Having been at the bottom with Bristol City, I can appreciate any success more than most.

"I don't think all the professionals in the Premiership realise just how lucky they are these days. They get highly paid whether they perform well or not.

"The players at Norwich are not in the high-earners bracket. But bonuses give us the extra incentive to keep chasing results.

"It always gave us an edge when we were playing the big-money teams, whether Manchester United, or Bayern Munich and Inter Milan in last season's UEFA Cup competition. Nothing gives players more pleasure than beating the big boys."

The good life came quite late for Newman. He'd played well over 400 games for Bristol City, winning the Freight Rover Trophy at Wembley in 1986, and proving himself one of the top defenders in the lower divisions.

"I was 27 before Norwich finally gave me the opportunity to prove what I could do in the top flight," says Rob.

"After all that time, I was beginning to think the chance had passed me by.

"Coming to Norwich gave me the opportunity to see if I really was good enough. If I hadn't signed for them, I would always have wondered what might have been.

"I know I'm not the greatest player in the Premier League, but I have at least proved I can survive at this level. But it took quite a while to do that.

"Despite all the experience I'd gained with Bristol City over the years, it still didn't prepare me for life at the top. In fact, it probably took me two years.

"I needed all that time to get used to the pace and speed of thought required. But after a couple of years trying to find my feet — and my best position — I finally felt I was good enough.

"The system that former Norwich boss Mike Walker used certainly brought the best out of my game. It allowed me to combine the main strengths of my game.

"In the past I'd been moved from centre-back to midfield and even played a few games up front. But the new sweeper system allowed me to play in a position that combined the role of centre-half and full-back. That suited me perfectly.

"More important than anything else was going out on the pitch and enjoying ourselves. After what I'd experienced earlier in my career, I was determined to make the most of it.

"If you can't enjoy playing at places like Munich's Olympic Stadium and the San Siro, you shouldn't be playing football. I'd love the chance to do all that again."

GARY McALLISTER

LEEDS UNITED

GARY McALLISTER has never figured on the list of the country's top scorers. But when the Leeds United and Scotland captain does get his name on the scoresheet, the chances are it has been the result of a spectacular strike.

The former Motherwell and Leicester City star has become a specialist in the art of hitting the net with long-range volleys and free kicks from outside the penalty area. However, he also includes a few tap-ins among his favourites.

Here, McAllister presents his ten most memorable goals.

1 April 13, 1985. Celtic 1 Motherwell 1.

It was a Scottish Cup semi-final at Hampden Park and I scored in the first half to put Motherwell ahead. Teammate Ronnie Blair had cut inside from the left flank and fired a shot which was parried by Celtic goalkeeper Pat Bonner. I slammed home the rebound from close range.

There was no degree of difficulty, but that remains one of my memorable goals because, along with winning the Scottish First Division a couple of times, reaching the semi-final of the cup was a big

highlight of my early career before moving to Leicester. Unfortunately, Celtic equalised and beat us 3-0 in the replay.

2 September 3, 1986. Leicester City 2 Liverpool 1.

This was one of my best deliveries from a free kick. We were awarded the kick just outside the penalty area and I managed to lift it perfectly over the wall and beyond Liverpool 'keeper Mike Hooper.

We actually led 2-0 in that game before Liverpool player-manager Kenny Dalglish brought himself on as a substitute and scored with one of his specialities — cutting in from the right and scoring with a left-foot bender. But we held on for the points.

3 October 24, 1987. Hull City 2 Leicester City 2.

Nothing spectacular about this goal, but I have included it because I scored with a header. Coming from me, that is a rare gem indeed.

The cross came from the right wing and I managed to nip in front of a Hull defender. I closed my eyes before getting in a glancing header from around the penalty spot. I was pleasantly surprised to see the ball nestling in the net.

With my height, maybe I should score more goals with my head, but I rarely get into the situations to do so.

4 May 7, 1988. Middlesbrough 1 Leicester City 2.

We went to Ayresome Park for

the last game of the season, with Middlesbrough needing a win to secure promotion from the old Second Division. We spoiled their party, although they later went up via the play-offs.

At half time, our manager David Pleat told me to have a few pops from long range during the second half because he'd noticed how deep they were sitting.

I took a pass from Peter Weir just inside the Boro' half. I ran on a couple of paces, then the ball took a lovely bobble which set it up perfectly. I let fly and, from 35 yards, it sailed past their 'keeper, Stephen Pears.

5 March 11, 1989. Manchester City 4 Leicester City 2.

Team-mate Paul Ramsey was in possession and I was positioned in the centre circle hoping the ball would come to me because I'd noticed City 'keeper Andy Dibble on the edge of his area, playing like a sweeper. It was a good situation to try and chip him.

Paul came through two tackles before the ball ran away from him and came in my direction. From just over the halfway line, I played the

10 **of**

lob which caught Andy by surprise and found the back of the net.

6 October 17, 1990. Scotland 2 Switzerland 1.

This was a qualifying match for the European Championships. We were already a goal up when, in the 53rd minute, Stuart McCall dinked a lovely ball over our opponents' defence for me to run on to from the right.

The Swiss thought I was offside, but the referee played on and I ran on to smash a volley low across the goalkeeper.

It turned out to be the decisive goal because Switzerland pulled one back later in the second half.

Just as important for me was the fact that it was my first goal for Scotland and I think every fan could tell from the broad smile on my face what a proud moment it was for me.

7 August 29, 1992. Leeds United 2 Liverpool 2.

We were the newly-crowned League Champions and had just set off in defence of our title, confident that we would once again be among the front-runners.

Early in the game, Lee Chapman set me up on the edge of the Liverpool penalty area. I took it on the volley, hit my shot cleanly and the ball beat goalkeeper David James high to his left.

Unfortunately, we were unable to sustain our League challenge during a very disappointing season in which we didn't manage a single away win.

8 September 30, 1992. Leeds United 4 VfB Stuttgart 1.

I had been fortunate to have scored with all the penalties I had taken for Leeds, but this was probably the most important of them all.

It was the second leg of our European Cup first round tie and, having lost 3-0 in Germany, nobody gave us a prayer of overturning the deficit.

But the Leeds support was magnificent that night. They provided a tremendous atmosphere and roared us on.

When we were awarded the penalty, I felt more pressure on me than I have at any other spot-kick. I was acutely aware of how important it was for me to score with it, and the goal seemed to shrink before my eyes.

But I placed my shot high to the goalkeeper's left and felt relief as much as joy to have scored.

After winning 4-1, we thought we had been knocked out on the away goals rule. But we later discovered that Stuttgart had fielded too many foreign players and UEFA ordered a replay in Barcelona, which we won 2-1.

9 October 21, 1992. Rangers 2 Leeds United 1.

Going back to Scotland to play in a European Cup match at Ibrox was a special occasion for me, and scoring in the first minute turned out to be a strange experience!

The Scottish fans hadn't seen much of me before my move from Motherwell to Leicester, so I'd been looking forward to putting in a good performance, especially as all my family were there to watch.

The noise was breathtaking. I'd never experienced noise like that at a football match before.

We won a corner on the left, and it was headed clear to just outside the penalty area, where I was waiting. I lashed a shot which flew into Andy Goram's top right-hand corner.

Ibrox suddenly went so quiet, at first I thought the referee must have given offside. It was eerie. Having been so ear-splitting, the match was played in a deathly hush until Rangers equalised in 26 minutes.

We eventually lost the tie 4-2 on aggregate.

10 February 28, 1994. Oldham Athletic 1 Leeds United 1.

I work very hard on my free kicks from around the edge of the penalty area. Most days after training, Gary Speed, Tony Dorigo and myself stay behind to practise our technique.

This goal was proof that practice makes perfect and it was very satisfying to see a free kick come off during a match having spent so many hours getting it right.

This one was from just a few yards outside the Oldham box. I wrapped my foot around the ball nicely and placed it right in the postage stamp to goalkeeper Jon Hallworth's right. I couldn't have squeezed it in closer to the angle.

Oldham manager Joe Royle blamed his 'keeper at first but, after watching it on video a few times, I think he acknowledged that Jon just couldn't get to it.

the best

ERIC CANTONA   **MANCHESTER UNITED**

LEE CLARK   **NEWCASTLE UNITED**

If there's one thing guaranteed to rile supporters of smaller clubs, it's seeing a star player leave for pastures new.

By that token, Queens Park Rangers fans have suffered more than most in recent years. They have had to watch star names like David Seaman, Paul Parker, Roy Wegerle and Darren Peacock move to big name sides, to the obvious disadvantage of their own team.

England internationalist Andy Sinton was another Loftus Road favourite who found himself firstly in demand and then on the move. He found himself with the choice of a move across London to join Arsenal or up the M1 to sign on for Sheffield Wednesday.

The exciting wide-man decided on a move back to his native north and made his Wednesday debut against Arsenal in August 1993. It wasn't until January of 1994, however, that he first found out how much losing him meant to the QPR faithful.

A New Year's Day return to his old Loftus Road stomping ground turned into an ordeal for Andy. The home fans gave him a hostile reception. They were fed up with losing top players and had come to believe that Andy had instigated his own move away.

"I did take a lot of stick from the stands and terraces that day," recalls Andy. "And I would be a liar if I said it didn't disappoint me at the time.

"Unfortunately, the people giving me the stick didn't really know the full story behind my move to Sheffield.

"I had been asked many times by journalists and the like to give my side of the story, but didn't because that isn't my style. With hindsight, though, maybe I should have done.

"When I left QPR, I was made out to be the one who wanted the transfer. That wasn't right. I never asked to leave the club.

"Rangers has always been a selling club. You only have to look at the players they sold over the few

● A tussle with Arsenal's Martin Keown. One day they might have been team-mates.

years before I left to see that.

"David Seaman went to Arsenal, Paul Parker to Manchester United and Roy Wegerle to Blackburn. Then Darren Peacock left for Newcastle a few months after I came to Wednesday.

"On gates of around 10 or 11,000 it's possible that they will always need to sell the occasional player to balance the books.

"However, I feel that to save themselves from criticism they tried to put a little bit of the blame on me.

"That's where I think the hostile reaction came from. People can only believe what they read.

"But my conscience was always clear. I knew then and know now that everything I did was right. The move was a typical move between two football clubs. There was nothing else in it.

"Sheffield Wednesday came in with a bid, QPR accepted it and I was on my way."

Although the initial reaction of Rangers supporters to the return of their former favourite was a let-down to England international Andy, happenings after the actual event cheered him greatly.

"The fans' reaction that day

disappointed me because I had four-and-a-half very happy years as a Rangers player," he goes on.

"I love the club, made a lot of friends, got on well with the supporters and have plenty of happy memories of my time as a player at Loftus Road.

"I have broad shoulders, so while I was disappointed at the reception, it didn't bother me too much. In the week following the game, though, I received literally hundreds of letters from QPR followers.

"The letters apologised for the way I had been treated on my return. They told me that I had given them years of great service. It was great to read such nice words.

"I'm a Sheffield Wednesday player now, though, and actually settled in at Hillsborough very quickly after my move, helped by the fact that this is a club with a real

"don blame

family atmosphere.

"I also knew the manager, Trevor Francis, who bought me for QPR as well as for Wednesday, and several of the players who I got to know on trips with the England national side.

"That meant I wasn't walking into a totally strange dressing room and helped me get quickly into my stride. I thought my early form for Wednesday was as good as it had ever been.

"Some Sheffield people were saying really good things about me and that even at £2.7 million I was a little bit of a bargain. It was great to hear such things soon after joining a new club."

Sheffield Wednesday's **ANDY SINTON** wants to put the record straight.

t me!"

A DAY WIT DIFFEREN

AIRDRIE'S **EVAN BALFOUR** HAS A DAILY ROUTINE
OTHER PLAYER. HERE'S A TYPICAL DAY IN THE LIFE
"FOOTBALLING FIREMAN"...

5am

● Goodbye, dear. Have a nice day. Wife Jenny is an air-hostess with Air UK, flying shuttles from Edinburgh to Stansted, Gatwick and Amsterdam. Early morning starts are par for the course in the Balfour household!

7am

● Playtime! There's no point in going back to bed — especially when one-year-old Hollie's awake!

3pm

● Evan HAS to keep his fitness up. Not just for football but also for his job as fireman with Lothian and Borders Fire Brigade.

TH A
CE
UNLIKE ANY
OF THE

noon

7pm

● Weight-watching! The Balfours have family membership of a local fitness club. Jenny and Hollie go for a swim — Evan goes for some fitness work, battling back from a medial ligament injury.

● Jenny's back from work so now it's time for lunch . . . (or is it breakfast?) and a read of the morning papers.

● Time for a family photograph before a bath for Hollie and an early night. Remember, the alarm goes off at 4.30 am!

8pm

● How Airdrie fans want to see Evan. Fit again, and spearheading their bid for promotion to the Premier League.

STRIKE IT

SOME people believe luck plays a big part in a footballer's success, and I admit I have been lucky over the past eighteen months.

My biggest piece of luck came in March 1993 when Kenny Dalglish signed me for Blackburn Rovers and ended my spell at Chelsea which had started to go downhill quickly. I was in and out of the team at Stamford Bridge and feeling pretty low, wondering when I was going to get a run in the side.

The manager at the time, Dave Webb, obviously didn't see me figuring in his plans and I often found myself playing for the reserves at Kingstonian's ground most weeks for Chelsea. I was obviously unhappy with things, but I knew I wasn't in a unique situation.

Everybody, no matter what they do, finds themselves in situations where they feel like they are hitting a brick wall and that's how I was feeling at Chelsea. Football isn't just about kicking a ball about every Saturday, there is more to it than that behind the scenes.

There are a lot of politics involved in the game and sometimes you have to accept you are in a situation similar to a one-way street, with no obvious way forward.

The fact that I was turning out for the reserves in front of low crowds at a non-league ground wasn't the problem. Nobody is too big to turn out for the reserves, but when you are treated like a nobody at your own club you feel let down and drained of all confidence.

It's then when you know your time is up. After playing with the club for a number of seasons, coming up through the ranks and getting experience, you expect it to count for something, but that wasn't the case.

As a player who came through the system at the club, I had a lot of feelings for it, but I knew I had to make a fresh start somewhere else. I felt I needed to get away to prove to myself that I was still a good player, and capable of fulfilling the promise I had shown in my early days at Stamford Bridge.

When I first broke into the Chelsea side as a 20-year-old, people were tipping me for stardom and it was nice to be acclaimed so much at an early stage of my career. Unlike some young players, I enjoyed the praise and didn't allow

● A FOOTBALLING FIRST! Graeme Le Saux becomes the first Channel Islander to play for England in April 1994.

it to affect my game.

I've always been a person who only worries about what I think about my game. I always try to play to the best of my ability, not to please the pundits, but to be happy with myself. I know I won't play well every game, and I also know that players rarely go through a game without making at least one mistake.

I just try to go out and play to my strengths and learn from previous mistakes. Whatever stage my game is at, I always feel there is room for improvement and I stick to that philosophy.

My desire to improve myself was part of the reason I was unhappy at Stamford Bridge. I was in a situation where I couldn't further myself by playing reserve team football and knew that I needed a new challenge.

In all fairness to Chelsea they knew that as well. Dave Webb was the person who sold me, but there are no grievances about that. I'm glad he saw me as an unhappy player and allowed me to leave to try to get my career going again.

That was my number one goal when I moved to Blackburn. It was difficult for me to leave Chelsea after spending all of my career with them. I'll always be grateful to the club for giving me my big chance, but I never felt sorry about leaving them for Rovers.

I saw the move as a chance to establish myself again and went to Ewood Park with such a strong will and desire to succeed that I was never going to regret leaving London.

Right from the start, I knew I had made the correct decision in moving to Blackburn. The Rovers manager, Kenny Dalglish, told me he had bought me to play at full-back and it was up to me to show I was worthy of a place in his team.

By telling me he wanted me for one position and one position only, he gave me an immediate boost to my confidence which had taken something of a battering during my time at Chelsea. It may sound strange, but it gave me an immediate feeling of security.

At Chelsea I was often used as a utility player who would play anywhere down the left hand side. I didn't enjoy being moved around all the time, but at least I was getting a game. My versatility wasn't the advantage some people would believe it to be, however.

I was unable to play in one position for any period of time and it left me feeling very vulnerable. Once the specialist left-back or left-midfielder returned I often found myself axed. I don't have that excuse at Blackburn and I'm glad about it.

The boost Kenny gave me in my early days at the club by telling me about his plans for me helped me to settle in quite easily. When I arrived, I felt a lot of pressure on myself to perform, and most of that pressure was self-inflicted because I saw all of the big names in the team and I was trying too hard to justify my

LUCKY!

How Blackburn banished the blues for Graeme Le Saux

place alongside them.

Things went well though, and my confidence was returning all the time. You can imagine how much it was lifted when I was lucky enough to be called up for England by Terry Venables in his first match in charge against the European Champions, Denmark.

The call-up capped an amazing year for me, but I was pessimistic about being selected right up to the moment the squad was announced. All the newspapers were saying I was a certainty to be called up, but I was cautious about it, wondering if I really would be included.

It was a great honour and once the news became definite I found myself at the centre of something of a media circus because of my connections with the Channel Islands after being born in Jersey.

Nobody from the Islands had ever represented England before and suddenly there was a chance two Channel Islanders could do so, as Matt Le Tissier, who was born in Guernsey, was also in the squad.

For both myself and Matt, the Channel Island connection was never really a factor, but the Media built it up as a race between Matt and I. I was more concerned about making a good impression for myself if I was lucky enough to be given a role from the start.

For the record, I beat Matt by sixty minutes to become the first Channel Islander to play for England, but that's just a nice extra. Playing for England is the best thing.

I've had a taste now and I want more, but Terry Venables was right when he said the only way the caps will keep coming is by performing for your club. I wouldn't have broken into the England side if it wasn't for my club form and that remains the priority.

My experience at Chelsea taught me that football is a hard game and things can change in a very short space of time, so I won't be taking things for granted.

In twelve months I went from being a Chelsea reserve going nowhere to an England international enjoying every minute of his football. My time at Chelsea may not have been very enjoyable in the final stages, but it taught me a lot about the game and I have taken it on board.

Success can be fleeting, but I hope my experience will help me to ensure that I don't take it for granted.

A DAY REME

NEWCASTLE UNITED

TODAY'S MATCH SPONSOR

TO MBER

● Man-of-the-Match with the Master-of-Memory! Steve Watson and David.

Six-year-old David Ebdale is Newcastle daft! He's turned his bedroom in Washington, Tyne and Wear into a shrine to his beloved Magpies — and turned himself into a walking encyclopaedia on Newcastle United!

David spends hours reading reports of Newcastle games, memorising all the match facts. He can rattle off who scored — and when. Who was booked — and why. He can even tell you the attendance and the referee's name!

There was one match where all those details spring to mind a little more easily. It was the Newcastle versus Swindon match in March 1994 when David was match mascot.

David had long dreamed of leading United out as mascot, but even he couldn't have dreamed of the scoreline — 7-1 to Newcastle! The scorers and times? No problem!

Beardsley (12, 70), Lee (27, 62), Watson (76, 79) Fox (84). Swindon's consolation goal came from Moncur (77). The crowd was 32,216 and the referee was Mr Reed!

David surprised everyone by correctly guessing the Man-of-the-Match (Steve Watson) and the time of the first goal (12 mins 5 seconds)!

After posing with the match officials and rival captains Beardsley and Taylor, David tested United keeper Pavel Srnicek with a few shots then took his seat in the stand with his Mum, Dad and Grandad.

Then it was downstairs for the post-match presentations — and more pictures for David's bedroom wall.

Dad Colin has to grin and bear his son's fanatical support for the Magpies. He's a fan of their local rivals Sunderland!

● Steve Watson scores v. Swindon.

THERE is always an element of risk when you sign for a new club in a different country, but there is little doubt in my mind that moving to Scotland and joining Rangers was one of the best things I have ever done.

Winning five trophies in the past two seasons and picking up Player of the Year awards from the football writers and my fellow professionals have justified my decision to go to Ibrox.

And who can forget our amazing European Champions League run a couple of years ago?

But it's not just on-field successes that have satisfied me.

My wife, Bev, and our kids, Emma, Lucy, Faye and Tom have all settled well in Scotland after our time in Italy with AC Milan and in France with Monaco.

That, to me, is very important.

I always said that by the time my eldest daughter Emma was 10, I was going to move back to Britain for the sake of her education.

By the time she was nine my family had been in Monaco for three years and I simply jumped at the chance of moving to Glasgow when the then manager Graeme Souness approached me in the summer of 1990.

Before leaving France, I'd had talks with two major English sides. But Graeme let me know just how big Rangers were and how hungry he was to make them even more successful.

I knew Graeme was a winner from our confrontations in England-Scotland games, English League matches and games in Italy.

In fact, his Sampdoria side stopped me from winning my only medal over there when they beat AC Milan in the Italian Cup Final.

My first few months at Ibrox didn't go as smoothly as I would have liked, however.

Because of injury, I hadn't played a competitive game for five months before my arrival and to make matters worse I picked up a groin strain in pre-season training.

When I did get into the team, Graeme opted to play me alongside Mo Johnston, with fans' favourite Ally McCoist on the bench. Naturally, that didn't go down well with the Ibrox legions.

To be honest, the reaction on the terraces cut no ice with me. Indeed, I didn't hear their booing and chanting half the time.

It took me a dozen or so games to get into my stride, but I always knew it would only be a matter of time before the punters began to appreciate me.

Everything seems to have snowballed since I won the fans over, but that's mainly due to the leadership of Walter Smith who took over when Graeme left for Liverpool in 1991.

During our relatively successful European campaign in season 92-93, Walter proved that he is one of the best bosses in today's game.

Cracking Europe has to be the biggest aim for a club of Rangers' stature.

After six years on the continent I think I can safely say that that is the type of arena every professional player wants to appear in.

Take it from me, when you're a player in the Italian First Division, you know what the big time is all about.

But even the worries of an Old Firm star in Glasgow are nothing compared to my experiences in Italy.

I've never come across people as fanatical about football as the Italians. And, while it was nice to

● Mark in his Monaco days

RANGERS' **MARK HATELEY** HAS HIS SIGHTS SET ON EUROPEAN GLORY

TARGET EURO

PE

GLASGOW

PORTSMOUTH

MILAN

MONACO

● Mark is one of the few players who
has played for clubs from four different countries.

play in front of such
appreciative crowds, I simply couldn't leave home
and go into town
without being mobbed.

As a result, my family
and I ended up spending
an incredible amount of
time inside our own
house, or else with the
family of Ray Wilkins, who
played alongside me at
the San Siro.

Going to Milan definite-
ly improved me as a play-
er because Serie A is
probably the best League
in the world.

I went over there when
I was just 21, and, at the
time, it was a great
upheaval because I was
already married with two
kids.

Monaco, however, was
an altogether more
relaxed affair.

It was difficult getting
used to playing in front of
crowds of 3000 after the
70,000 who regularly
attended the Italian matches.

I had to keep myself
motivated by regarding it

as a new challenge. And,
at the end of my first season there, I won a French
Championship medal.

The lifestyle also made
a refreshing change. From
being penned in at Milan, I
could walk around
Monaco to my heart's con-
tent.

With a population of
just 28,000 the principality
is like a big village and,
because of the wealth
there, they have the
Formula One Grand Prix
plus some top tennis tour-
naments.

It was all very nice, but
when the chance came up
to return to Britain —, and
Rangers — I didn't hesi-
tate.

Now I've signed a deal
at Ibrox that should keep
me here until the end of
my career.

I'm enjoying my football
more so than at any other
stage in my life and if
Rangers carry on winning
on the domestic front and
make further inroads in
Europe, then I'll be more
than happy.

MARK HATELEY   **RANGERS**

ROBBIE EARLE   **WIMBLEDON**

THE BOOT-ROOM BOY

On February 5, 1994 a local boy really did make good. Roy Evans, born in the Liverpool suburb of Bootle in 1948, sent out his very own Liverpool team to face Norwich City at Carrow Road.

Being involved with the Anfield club was certainly nothing new to Roy. At that time, two thirds of his life had been spent on the Liverpool payroll as player, reserve team coach and assistant manager.

But he took charge against the Canaries as manager after succeeding former big-name boss Graeme Souness, who had relinquished the position following a humiliating home FA Cup defeat at the hands of First Division Bristol City.

But while some may have seen replacing a household name like Souness with a relative unknown such as Evans as a bold step, those in the know at Anfield were confident of the results.

Liverpool have a history of putting club men in the manager's chair. After Bill Shankly had led the famous club out of mediocrity and into football's top bracket, loyal club men such as Bob Paisley, Joe Fagan and Kenny Dalglish carried on the success.

Graeme Souness may not have moved up through the ranks like his three predecessors, but he had, of course, been a player there. He couldn't, however, continue the club's unique run of success.

It has been left to Roy Evans, Liverpool through and through, to put the club back on the trophy-winning trail. And if he manages it, then add his name to the Anfield roll of honour.

"Before taking over as manager I worked underneath Graeme Souness and know for a fact that he worked very hard to make this club successful.

"The fact things didn't work out as he would have liked certainly wasn't down to a lack of effort on his part, it was probably just not to be. Like him, though, I am judged on results.

"I wouldn't have taken the manager's job if I didn't expect to win things. That would have been pointless.

"I've been asked if becoming manager here is a dream come true. Well, it's PART of the dream. The other part is to be successful and to win things.

"I must admit, though, that the first thing I found difficult about being a manager was winning. The hardest things about the job all concern the football. It's the part we all enjoy the most, but also the most important part.

"It was said that people in the Press had the knives out for Graeme when he was manager. I'm disappointed when I hear that.

"Personally, I haven't found the

Prior to taking the job, many football fans would have known Roy's face from television coverage of him sitting on the Liverpool bench, but may not have known his name.

Despite being associated with the club for so long, until becoming team boss he had remained relatively anonymous.

A graduate of the famous Anfield boot room, the cramped room where the Liverpool coaching staff devised the club's all-conquering tactics, Roy has been a coach for more than half of his life.

But were it not for those fine teachers Bill Shankly, Bob Paisley and Joe Fagan, his coaching abilities could well have been lost to the game.

"I came to the club as a player at 15, straight from school," he goes on. "That was in 1964, under Mr Shankly.

"My career progressed from there — slowly. I played a lot of Central League games for the reserve team, although I only made nine first-team appearances. I suppose I just wasn't good enough to hold down a spot.

"Bill Shankly retired when I was 25. It was then that Bob Paisley asked me if I would take the job of reserve team coach.

"At that age all you want to do is play football, so I turned the chance down three or four times. It was only after a lot of persuasion that I finally agreed to take it.

"It has turned out to be a more successful side of my career than playing, so I have benefited from that early baptism.

"Had I not taken the club up on that offer there is always the chance that I would have moved on from Liverpool, although I was never really keen to go anywhere else.

"There were one or two offers and I suppose I might have gone if something attractive had come up. Fortunately it didn't, but I did go on loan — to Philadelphia in America.

"I really enjoyed my spell over there and actually won the American League title. That's one medal none of the players here have won.

"Whenever they try and wind me up by asking to see all my medals, I ask them to show me their American Championship medal!

"On returning from the States, I was offered the job of reserve-team manager. With the reserves, you may be under the manager of the first-team, but are still the boss of your own little team.

"Most of the time it was a one-man job but I enjoyed being trainer, manager and coach over the eleven or so years I had in the post."

Eight Central League titles in nine years confirmed Roy's quality and proved he had learnt from Anfield greats like Shankly and Paisley.

Now, playing for higher stakes, it is a mix of ideas which Evans is using in his efforts to propel Liverpool back towards the top.

"You must keep your own personality in the job, but you must also listen to people around you. It isn't a myth or a legend that managers and coaches here learn from their predecessors, it's common sense.

"You always respect what people with great experience say, but you don't necessarily have to agree with it. Football is all about opinions and you must keep your own as they are on what you will ultimately be judged.

"The basis of football here has always been the same. People have always wanted to play the Liverpool way, but they have put the ideas over in different ways.

"I suppose what is being implemented now is a mix of what has gone before. The game has changed a lot over 30 years, but the basics remain the same.

"There are a lot of facets to football, but it's mainly about being able to pass the ball, control it and move. I learnt that at an early age and nobody has tried to change it.

"There is a lot of talk these days about long-ball football. Even when we play there is a place in the game for someone hitting the ball 60 yards.

"I won't stop that, I just don't think every ball should be hit such a long way. I want to see a variety of all kinds of passes."

Press any problem. I believe you have to talk to them but don't have to tell them everything.

"We have a big following fan-wise and they deserve to have some idea of what is happening. At the same time, they shouldn't know everything because there are ways of doing certain things which need to be kept on the secretive side.

"On the whole, there isn't much difference between being manager of a side and being assistant manager. The biggest difference, of course, is that the buck now stops with me when it comes to team selection.

"I will still ask people for their opinions and will listen to them, but after considering all the options I will say, 'this is the team I am picking.'

"I've been here a very long time and always hoped I would get the job. When Graeme resigned I thought I must have a chance. The offer was made and I was glad to accept it."

backing

JOHN ALDRIDGE—
Tranmere Rovers — hopes that he can be a success off the pitch as well as on it!

GED BRANNAN

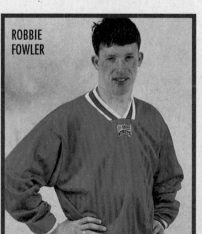

ROBBIE FOWLER

WHEN footballers reach the day when they have to hang up their boots, many are faced with the prospect of a life outside the game which has been their livelihood for so long.

John Aldridge will have no such problems though. If, in the unlikely event he doesn't find himself with a top management job, he can always turn to the football kit manufacturing company of which he is a director!

Tranmere and Republic of Ireland striker Aldridge has been part of the company, US Athletic, since the end of the 1992-93 season and sees it as something he can fall back on if things don't go to plan for him.

John reveals, "At the end of the 1993 season, a couple of friends of mine, Warren Gavin and Brian Omar, approached me to see if I'd be interested in becoming a director in US Athletic.

"For quite a few years it had been a leisure business, but they were branching out into the replica kit trade. After speaking to the lads and making one or two phone calls I decided it was a good proposition and became a fully paid up partner.

"It was important to me that the kits were of a good standard because I didn't want to tarnish my reputation by getting involved with sub-standard products. After seeing the kits though, I had no worries because they were of a high standard and was confident I was back-

a winner!

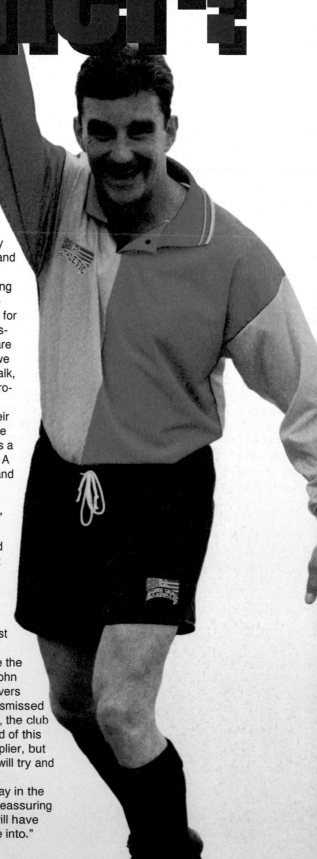

ing a winner.

"When I became involved, Brian and Warren were busy researching the market, mainly around Merseyside and Southern Ireland. With my name involved with the company it was obvious these were the places to target.

"There is a very big market for these kits, particularly in Ireland, and if we go about it the right way we can make a foothold for ourselves and build up a reputation.

"At the moment we are concentrating our efforts on supplying amateur teams, but we have already managed to get a GM Vauxhall Conference team to wear our gear.

"Runcorn wore our kits during the 1993-94 season and their response has been great. They are very happy with the kits. If we can continue to supply Runcorn and get some other non-league sides on board it will be a good start.

"Hopefully, in time, we can supply Football League clubs. We aren't kidding ourselves about the business though. We know we will never

be able to compete with the likes of Umbro or Adidas, we just want to make our own niche in the market.

"Things are looking promising over in Ireland, and in some ways I have to thank Roy Keane, Ronnie Whelan and Steve Staunton for that.

"When we were printing our first catalogue, these lads all modelled the kits for us which was a great gesture. The three of them are from all over Ireland so we managed to cover Dundalk, Dublin and Cork in the process!

"Seriously though, their presence in the catalogue is a boost and it gives us a good chance over there. A couple of League of Ireland teams have already expressed an interest in wearing US Athletic kits."

Aldridge has also enlisted team-mates Ged Brannan, Eric Nixon, Pat Nevin and Liam O'Brien along with Liverpool's Robbie Fowler and Manchester City's Terry Phelan to model the latest kits.

"I'm trying to convince the manager at Tranmere, John King, to let us supply Rovers with kits and he hasn't dismissed it. At the moment though, the club is contracted until the end of this season with another supplier, but when that deal is up we will try and get something done.

"Although I want to stay in the game when I retire, it is reassuring to know that if I don't, I will have something to put my time into."

TRADITION, family pressure, relegation and a retirement all had a hand in Nottingham Forest losing their most valuable asset at the end of season 1992-93.

Midfield maestro Roy Keane had spent several happy seasons at the City Ground since moving from the Republic of Ireland as a raw 18-year-old.

But when Forest dropped to the First Division two seasons ago and manager Brian Clough decided to call it a day, Keane made it known he was on his way out of Forest.

A posse of big clubs showed an interest, but the huge transfer fee frightened off all but Manchester United and Blackburn Rovers.

Keane was a United supporter as a boy and comes from a family of Reds fans. The club's tradition and awesome potential made his decision to choose Old Trafford a formality.

But Keane admits that things could have been so different if Forest hadn't been relegated and Clough had stayed at the City Ground.

When Forest lost their boss and top-flight status, Keane was just a couple of months into a lucrative three-and-half year contract which contained a 'get-out' clause in the event of relegation.

Keane has never hidden his admiration for Cloughie and it is unlikely he would have exercised his right to leave if the former Forest boss had remained in charge.

But Cloughie's successor, Frank Clark, admits it took him just ten seconds to realise that the departure of Clough and the prospect of First Division football had made up Keane's mind.

"If Forest hadn't been relegated, I would have stayed," Keane confesses.

"But it was Brian Clough's departure that had a huge bearing on my decision. I would probably have played in the First Division last season if Brian was still in charge.

"I can just picture us having a chat in his office at the end of the season. He is very persuasive and probably would have talked me round. He was always good at doing that!

That's Manchester United's ROY KEANE

○ What Roy might have looked like if Kenny Dalglish had got his way!

"I had a brilliant three years at Forest and I owe Brian Clough everything. As far as my football career is concerned, I am what I am because of Brian.

"I could have seen myself spending the rest of my career at Forest if circumstances had been different. I had signed a three-and-a-half year contract and would have honoured it."

Although Cloughie may have persuaded Keane to stay, Clark was unable to prevent him moving on.

"I had a talk with the new manager and told him I couldn't afford to spend a season in the First Division.

"I wanted to play in the World Cup at the end of last season and my chances would have been reduced if I was in a lower division.

"Some people said to me that I should just stick it out at Forest and I would probably still get a game with Ireland. But that wasn't the issue.

"I know in my own mind that I wouldn't have improved at Forest. In the First Division I would have been at a standstill.

"It was better for Forest and myself that I should have left. The £3.75m fee was good business for the club. After all, I only cost them £10,000 from Cobh Ramblers.

"I don't feel I was jumping ship. I like to think I didn't really have a choice but to leave. Forest needed to strengthen their squad and my leaving gave them money to spend.

"They spent over £3m on Colin Cooper from Millwall and Stan Collymore from Southend. They are proving to be big assets."

Once it became clear Forest were set to lose Keane, big-spending Blackburn Rovers entered the picture and appeared to clinch a deal for the 23-year-old.

But this presented a dilemma for Keane. His family are staunch United fans and he also supported the Reds as a boy in Ireland.

"It's not just my immediate family who support United. It's also aunts and uncles. In fact, I think every second person in Ireland follows Manchester United."

"If I had left the decision to my family, I would probably have come to United long before now. So when I decided to leave Forest, they made it clear there was only one club for me.

"I had my hands full last season trying to get enough tickets to go round them all."

His boss at Old Trafford, Alex Ferguson, knew that despite the attentions of other clubs, Keane had his heart set on being a United player.

Fergie commented, "The lad was always determined to come here and I'd wanted him since he played for Forest against us three years ago.

"He could have gone to Blackburn and earned more money, but that's the magic of United."

Ferguson's reference to the financial aspect of the deal strikes a chord with Keane's attempt to set the record straight on accusations that he was being 'greedy' during the transfer dealings.

Initially, it was his former boss Clough who claimed he was asking for too much money while negotiating his last Forest contract.

These claims seemed to stick with Keane in his dealings with Blackburn and Manchester United.

"Money was never an issue with me," Roy adds. "I look upon this as a career move. The financial side never came into the equation.

"If I was greedy, I would have gone to Blackburn. It's common knowledge they offered better personal terms.

"All the talk about greed is just water off a duck's back as far as I'm concerned. I did nothing wrong.

"I've nothing against Kenny Dalglish and Blackburn Rovers. I'm pleased they showed an interest in me.

"But as soon as United came in, I made up my mind I was going to Old Trafford.

"I knew a lot about the club but I was still impressed with the way Alex Ferguson sold it to me. I had a gut feeling this was the right move.

"Alex Ferguson doesn't settle for second best. He has a great enthusiasm for the game and keeps talking about trophies and winning medals.

"I'm involved with this club because of their tradition and what they are achieving. There is no limit to what we can do here."

United's £3.75m buy broke the English transfer record, but Keane refused to accept that it heaps pressure on him to perform.

"The price tag is not a weight on my shoulders. In fact, I don't even think about it.

"I set my own standards and as long as I can match them, I'll be satisfied."

ROY KEANE

MEET

Some fans dream of meeting their idols. For most of them, it's only a dream — for others it can be reality. Perhaps a quick autograph after a match or if they're really lucky, a chance meeting while on holiday can result in a photograph which takes pride of place back home.

One man makes a habit of it, 40-year-old Andrew Hill from Highbridge, near Taunton. You name 'em and he's met 'em!

"I started all this back in 1967 when I used to collect pin-ups and player profiles from newspapers, magazines and the "Topical Times". Then I thought it would be nice to get them autographed by the players concerned. After that, the idea of being photographed with players came to me and

it's sort of taken off!"

Born in Stranraer, Andrew moved south at an early age, settling in Coventry. He became a keen Coventry fan but it was the mercurial talents of Messrs Best, Law and Charlton that caught

his eye.

"I can't say I'm a Manchester United supporter but I have to say that my favourite ground is Old Trafford and my favourite player was George Best."

Naturally, his picture with Best takes pride of place in a room devoted to his hobby, with the walls covered in pictures, posters and, of course, photographs.

BREAKFAST WITH BEST
LUNCH WITH LAW
DINNER WITH DEMPSEY

His travels have often found him arriving at his "target's" house at unusual

THE STARS

hours but more often than not he has been given a warm welcome.

"I try to phone beforehand to warn them of my arrival but if I happen to be in the area they simply say 'Come along'. Johnny Giles offered me a cup of tea and left me to look at his medal collection while his wife drove him to the station! Geoff Hurst took me out to lunch when he was down in the West Country and ex-Chelsea favourite John Dempsey invited me for dinner!"

Andrew works in the motor trade, which is just as well considering the thousands of miles he has clocked up. He once travelled as far as Aberdeen to meet John

Blackley! For Derek Dougan it was tenth time lucky — fifteen months were spent on this one. He's met all the Celtic Lisbon Lions and all the great Rangers players of the 60's. One particular feat was meeting twelve

ex-Scottish internationalists in one day! Meetings have taken place in strange venues — Barlinnie Prison, Glasgow, where Ian Ure was a social worker and the fish and chip shop of ex-England star John

Connelly!

"By now I must have over 3000 pictures and photographs in my collection plus countless scrapbooks. Luckily, my wife Lauren is quite keen, too, and often travels with me, camera at the ready!"

Andrew spends quite a lot of time researching the whereabouts of players. His endeavours have often resulted in putting old friends back in touch after many years lost contact.

Now Andrew sees a new challenge on the horizon . . .

"There are quite a number of stars' sons playing now, like Mike Summerbee's son Nicky of Swindon Town. Maybe I could start a 'Father and Son' collection!"

action-rep

I can't help but reflect on what an eventful first season it turned out to be for me at Celtic.

Three different managers, a boardroom take-over and ending up as top scorer ensured there was never a dull moment.

It's been a real roller-coaster ride, although I've already got used to highs and lows in my career.

Considering that, just seven-and-a-half years ago, I never thought I had a future in the game, you won't hear me complaining.

At that time I was with Blackpool, where I never managed to establish myself and only played in a dozen League games during a two-year spell.

My confidence was definitely low when Alex Miller came in to rescue the situation by signing me for Hibs in the summer of 1987.

Even then, my feeling was that if I couldn't make the breakthrough at Bloomfield Road, then my prospects for first-team football elsewhere were slim.

But after that initial self-doubt, the encouragement of Alex eventually led to me making the breakthrough. I'll be forever indebted to him for that.

I had six happy years at Hibs although typically for me, the highlight came a few months after my footballing future was again threatened.

It was the summer of 1991 when the team's financial problems looked set to result in the break-up of the club, with talk of even a merger with our city rivals Hearts.

The players were left in the dark by events because we weren't training regularly, but many of the Edinburgh-based lads did their bit to help the cause in what was an especially difficult time for them.

The supporters organised a rally, as well as a protest march, to show just how much Hibs meant to them.

When local businessmen joined the Board with the cash needed to keep the club alive, the sense of pride was evident in everyone concerned with it.

There was a real feeling amongst the players of pulling together when we re-started the new campaign, and that spirit played a major part in us reaching

● Fergus McCann — the man behind the Celtic revival.

the Skol Cup final three months later.

Our 2-0 win over Dunfermline that Sunday in September was effectively the best way we could thank the fans for the huge part they played in saving us.

Having experienced another take-over this season, I hope that lightning strikes twice for me and a similar turnaround in Celtic's fortunes occurs.

It was difficult to have the team's financial worries hanging over us in the early part of last season.

The difference was that, unlike at Hibs, we heard all sorts of rumours every day of what was happening at Parkhead.

The sheer size of the club brought home too just what a dramatic position we were in.

We weren't helped by results on the park, where our early form saw the departure of Liam Brady with Frank Connor temporarily in charge before Lou Macari took over as manager.

The fans were upset with what was going on, but again it was clear

their number one concern was saving the club.

After Fergus McCann came to take charge of the new Board in March, we all received a massive lift and felt united in going forward.

A feeling of real optimism swept over the club, just as I had experienced at Hibs.

The first game after his arrival was a real gala day when we travelled up to Perth to face St Johnstone, and won 1-0.

It was just another occasion where I realised I'd made the right move even though I was forced to leave the 'party' early with a back injury.

The rest of the team headed to Ireland for a short tour after the game, but the doctor ordered me to spend four days in bed to cure the problem, caused by a blood clot on a nerve at the base of my spine.

But despite that I was still able to appreciate just how much the take-over had meant to the supporters.

My wife Margaret's family, who are mad on Celtic, all phoned the house wanting to talk about it when I was laid up!

From a personal point of view, when I signed, I was concerned about the step-up that I was making.

Having failed at Blackpool, it was hard not to experience at the back of my mind some anxiety about joining such a big club.

But I scored in our opening two League Cup matches against

1888·

THAT'S WHAT CELTIC'S
PAT McGINLAY
WANTS!

Stirling Albion and Arbroath in the first month and felt that helped me settle down.

It also helped that throughout the season I was playing alongside a former Hibs team-mate, John Collins, in midfield.

As well as being familiar with his style of play, it helped knowing that he had made a success of the same move a few seasons earlier.

Finishing up as top scorer was something I consider a real honour. It's a team game, but I was pleased with the contribution I made.

While nobody's promising trophies at Parkhead just yet, I guarantee Celtic fans that the best is yet to come from me.

● Phil Brookes, football artist.

all his

Phil Brookes is a football artist specialising in oil paintings of the players, characters and events throughout soccer history.

Each of his pictures is researched in detail to capture the style and personality of the subject, and to recreate the atmosphere of the period; whether it be Pele in the heat of the Azteca Stadium from the 1970 World Cup, or Billy Meredith speeding goalwards under the gaze of Manchester's factory chimneys before the first World War. Phil's subjects hail from the modern game's Victorian beginnings to the present day: Dixie Dean to Stanley Matthews, Billy Walker with Villa's 1920 F.A. Cup, to Brian Clough, painted just prior to retirement from his glorious reign at Forest.

All the work is original and can be painted to commission if you have a personal favourite player or match, however famous or otherwise!

"What the customer gets is a picture they won't have seen anywhere before, one that will be an investment and I hope bring a bit of history alive for them," says Phil.

The formula works particularly well for the older themes where relatively few black and white images remain, so the colour and scale can help the viewer feel something of what it was like to 'be there'.

Phil's work is a unique way to commemorate an award ceremony or anniversary, and a picture of Mark Hateley was given to the player by a Rangers Supporters Club as a Player of the Year presentation.

Phil himself was brought up on the great Spurs sides of the sixties, and his stock catalogue includes canvasses of his boyhood hero John White plus other contemporary artists of the pitch such as Jim Baxter, Denis Law and Danny Blanchflower. He has shown his paintings at Wembley and Anfield (where they were part of the centenary celebrations), and produces the Christmas card design for the Football League.

Working from his Northampton studio, Phil continues, "The game has a long and proud history which is perhaps not well enough catered for in terms of a central museum site for instance, but there's a growth of interest in nostalgia at grassroots level, in books and videos and so on, and I hope my paintings will make a useful and interesting contribution."

own work !

A CLUB OR COUNTRY CHOICE FOR CRYSTAL PALACE'S
CHRIS ARMSTRONG

Celebration time !
Crystal Palace - Division
One champions.

Hot shot striker Chris Armstrong turned his back on the chance to play in the World Cup to make sure Crystal Palace returned to the Premiership in style.

The prolific young goal-scorer was wanted by Nigeria to play in the African Nations Cup — an offer that could have given him his passport to the United States for the World Cup itself.

It was a tough decision to make but, encouraged by Palace boss Alan Smith, Chris decided to put club before country. Even when Nigeria went on to win the tournament, he realised he'd made the right choice — especially when Terry Venables called him up to the England B squad at the end of the season.

"Going to the African Nations Cup could have cost me six or seven League games at a vital time of the season," says Armstrong. "I was pleased to see Nigeria win but I knew it would have cost me to have gone out there.

"Promotion was my priority last season. Nothing less would do after the bitter disappointment of the season before.

"We had been relegated on goal difference and that hurt everybody at the club. Steve Coppell resigned and Alan Smith was left to put things back together again.

"He couldn't have done a better job for us. Right from the start of last season he made sure that every-

thing was just right.

"His first step was to take the squad off to Portugal in pre-season. There we were put through a series of physical tests to make sure we were in perfect shape for the new season. I think the whole squad came through that with flying colours and we were all set for a good season.

"But the boss wanted to make sure we were also in good mental condition for the campaign. So he used a couple of psychologists to watch how players prepared themselves for each game.

"Everybody is different in that respect. We all have our own way of getting our minds straight for a game.

"It actually took us a couple of games to get everything going. Then, good wins against Nottingham Forest and Portsmouth helped us click into gear.

"The Portsmouth game was very special for me because I scored a hat-trick. That set me on the way to what was a great season.

"I'd actually scored fifteen goals in my first season at Palace after my transfer from Millwall. But they all counted for nothing when we were relegated.

"I was determined my goals were going to mean more to the team second time around. That certainly proved to be the case."

The only problem for Chris early on last season came about when he was sent-off in the Anglo-Italian Cup. It was to teach him a harsh lesson — he was developing a reputation as a top striker and that made him a marked man.

"Being dismissed in such an unimportant game was ridiculous," admits Chris. "It meant I had to sit out three games when I was just hitting top form in front of goal.

"That incident showed me that I had to stay cool and out of trouble. I must always keep my emotions under control.

"Just one moment of madness can mean a red card. That's no good to me or the team.

"Alan Smith makes sure that I concentrate on doing my job of scoring goals for Palace. I knew with him around we were heading in the right direction.

"The club was very low when Alan first took over. But he picked everybody up and got us all buzzing again.

"With Alan in charge I had no doubts about committing my future to Crystal Palace. There were supposed to be Premiership clubs intrested in me but I was very confident that Palace would soon be back playing with the big boys too. So I signed a new contract last season to keep me at the club for a while yet."

Despite Palace's impressive start last season, Alan Smith didn't shy away from blasting his players when necessary. If he didn't think they had played well, he'd tell them so.

"There are always times when a manager has to have a go at his players," says Chris. "I'm sure we deserved it at times, even during such a great season.

"Players react differently to the manager giving them a rocket. Personally I don't mind as long as it does the job.

"Alan is the man in charge and we've got to give him a lot of credit for everything he's done at Palace. He had to make the decisions — and thankfully most of them were right.

"One of his best was bringing Paul Stewart here on loan last season. Paul had been struggling to make an impression at Liverpool but he made all the difference to us.

"What a great partner he was for me during the last three months of the season. He has so much experience and that extra class which really showed through at Division 1 level.

"Paul's strong, holds the ball up well and I couldn't have hoped for a better partner. He gets the credit for a lot of my goals during that period.

"As soon as promotion and the Division 1 championship was secured I was looking forward to having another go at Premiership defenders. I learnt a lot about my business last season and I couldn't wait to prove myself against the best.

"Playing at the top level again gives me another chance to get international recognition. But second time around it's England, not Nigeria, I'm out to impress."

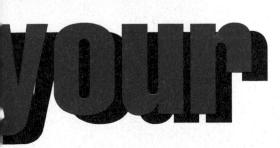

your pick

ANDY TOWNSEND   **ASTON VILLA**

JASON LEE   NOTTINGHAM FOREST

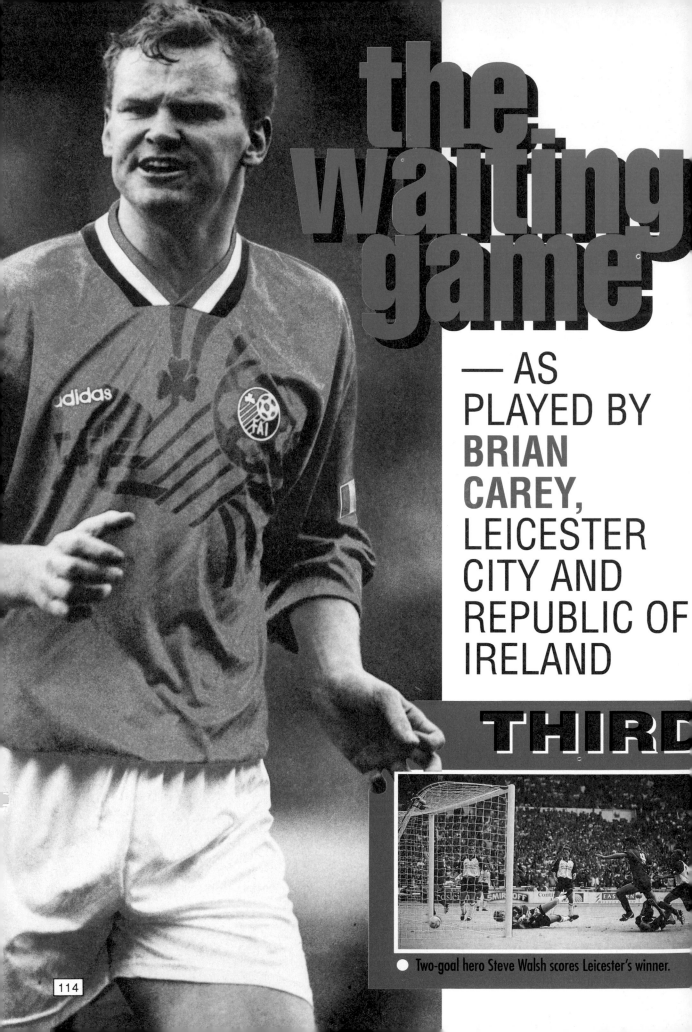

the waiting game

— AS PLAYED BY **BRIAN CAREY**, LEICESTER CITY AND REPUBLIC OF IRELAND

THIRD

● Two-goal hero Steve Walsh scores Leicester's winner.

LEICESTER CITY defender Brian Carey must have wondered if he would ever make a first-team appearance!

The 25-year-old spent five frustrating seasons at Champions Manchester United but never played in the first team.

He eventually managed 16 on-loan appearances at lowly Wrexham, including the Welsh club's stunning FA Cup Third Round victory over Arsenal in 1992.

You can only imagine his disappointment and disillusion at failing to register a first-team opportunity at Old Trafford.

Brian waited on the sidelines while younger players such as Lee Sharpe and Ryan Giggs rose through the ranks and passed him on the way to the big time.

So there are not many players who would admit a sense of relief when they part company with the Champions, but that's how Brian feels when he reflects on his United career.

"I could have got myself into a real rut if I'd stayed at Old Trafford. I could have made do with just picking up the wages every week and just putting up with things.

"But I have a lot more ambition than that and, though I'd been at the club for four years, I spent the last year on a week-to-week contract, anxious to get away and play regularly in somebody's first team.

"It was always a regret that I didn't establish myself in the United first team, but I have some fond memories of the club.

"A lot of players leave clubs determined to prove to their old manager that they were wrong not to put them into their first team.

"United were great to me and I owe them a lot. If it wasn't for them I may have gone back home to Ireland or down to London and tried a new career as a quantity surveyor.

"I served a three-year contract at Old Trafford and stayed for another year. I got a lot of help from the coaching staff, particularly Jim Ryan, who guided me through some rough times when things weren't going my way.

"I think there were a lot of people upset, apart from myself, when I was allowed to leave the club. But there is no bitterness towards United boss Alex Ferguson.

"He told me that I had a future in the game and to go out there and show that my four-year education at United wasn't wasted.

"I have no desire to show Manchester United anything this season. I simply want to prove to myself that I can be a success.

"I was a regular in the City side at the start of last season but I damaged ankle ligaments in a Coca-Cola Cup-tie at Rochdale.

"That kept me out for six matches, but I managed a place on the bench when we later met United in the competition.

"I was desperate to get on the pitch because I've never experienced playing in front of a big crowd at Old Trafford, despite spending so much time on their books.

"But that United jinx struck again and I never got a chance to show the home fans what I could do.

"My form was up and down before December and even though I recovered from the injury I was left out of the side. I can't blame the boss for leaving me out."

Carey admits that the upheaval which accompanied his move from Manchester to Leicester caught up with him after the initial novelty wore off.

Apart from moving house, he was also planning his wedding last December and reflects that perhaps his mind wasn't entirely on football.

He was dropped by manager Brian Little just before his wedding and left to wonder about his City future. He jokes: "The secret is not to get married during the season.

"I think Brian felt my mind was elsewhere. I was upset to be left out, but he probably did the right thing.

"Apart from the wedding, I was moving house to Leicester. It's such a big time in anyone's life and I may have had too much on my plate.

"But that was the way I chose to do it, and although I regret the dip in form, I wouldn't change very much.

"I feel that recently I've begun to make my mark at Leicester. Now that all the planning and upheavels are behind me, I'm more relaxed and happier than at any other time."

TIME LUCKY!

● Steve Walsh.

● Premiership here we come!

Brian and his Leicester team-mates won promotion to the Premiership via the play-offs at the third attempt. Blackburn and Swindon had foiled them on previous occasions. An exciting play-off final last May at Wembley saw Leicester beat Derby County 2-1, and put the Filbert Street side back among the big guns.

Why every game's the same for Chelsea's CRAIG BURLEY

CRAIG BURLEY was Chelsea's Mr Superstition on the way to last season's FA Cup Final.

The young Scottish midfielder got into the lucky habit of scoring goals in the first three rounds of the competition against Barnet, Sheffield Wednesday and Oxford United — and was very disappointed not to keep that run going.

Chelsea's Peter Osgood was the last player to score in every FA Cup round when the Blues won the Cup in 1970. And when the goals started to go in for Craig Burley last season, he had his eye on that record.

"I have to admit I was very disappointed when my scoring run came to an end in the quarter-finals," says Craig. "But at least I did get an assist for Gavin Peacock's winning goal.

"People don't really think of me as a goalscorer but I've always thought I can get my fair share. The goals I scored in the Cup certainly weren't a surprise to me, even if I did hit a couple with my weaker left foot.

"Like everything else I did during that cup run, scoring had become

match ritual

part of a lucky routine. Even when I missed out against Wolves, I kept the other superstitions going through to the Final.

"I always put on my shirt last when getting changed for a game and I was the last to run out of the tunnel as well.

"Another routine I got into before a match was to have a massage. We're lucky at Chelsea to have a top-class masseur in Terry Byrne.

"He does a great job in preparing players for a big game. We're all nice and relaxed after we've had a massage."

Craig is one of a very strong Scottish contingent at Stamford Bridge, including John Spencer, Steve Clarke and David Hopkin. But, unlike them, he never actually played in his home country.

"I never played competitive football in Scotland," says Craig.

"I was spotted by Chelsea when I was playing local football in Ayrshire.

"I always wanted to come to England when I was young because there wasn't really any competitive youth football in Scotland. It was hard to get the necessary experience back home.

"Ever since I've been at Chelsea, there has always been a strong Scottish flavour at the club. But it has never been a clique, even though we do get a share of stick from the other players.

"Fellow Scot Steve Clarke has always been a big help to me on and off the field. He has always had a word of advice if I needed it and last season we developed a very strong partnership down the right-hand side.

"Steve is a very dangerous player when he goes on one of his runs. He can frighten the life out of defenders when he gets going.

"That partnership very nearly came to an abrupt end last season when I was close to joining Coventry City. In fact, I was 95% certain that I was moving on.

"Glenn Hoddle didn't have a regular place for me at Chelsea at the time and going to Coventry looked like a good move. The deal was almost agreed but then Bobby Gould resigned as Coventry manager and it was all over.

"I was very disappointed but things soon picked up for me at Stamford Bridge. Going to Wembley at the end of the season showed how it turned around for me."

Craig wasn't the first Burley to play in the FA Cup Final. His uncle George had been in the winning Ipswich Town team in 1978.

"I can remember sitting through hours of videos with my family watching George win the cup. After that, I always wanted to play in the FA Cup Final myself," he says.

"Every player wants to play in the FA Cup Final — and that includes the Scots. The Scottish Cup just doesn't compare with the glamour of the FA Cup.

"We lost to Manchester United in last season's Final. But at least we all had the chance to savour a great occasion."

CRAIG'S FELLOW-SCOTS AT STAMFORD BRIDGE —
Steve Clarke, David Hopkin and John Spencer.

GARRY FLITCROFT   **MANCHESTER CITY**

SIMON DONNELLY   **CELTIC**

heads

Coventry City's **SEAN FLYNN** takes the aerial route to goal

I win

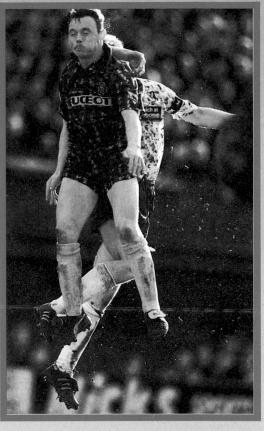

HE may stand at a modest 5 ft 8 ins, but Sean Flynn is an absolute giant when it comes to prowess in the air.

With the possible exceptions of Leeds United's Gary Speed and QPR ace Les Ferdinand, Flynn is the Premier League's top jumper.

The Coventry City winger-cum-striker doesn't know for sure where his terrific leaping ability was developed, but it's possible his skills were honed on the building sites of the West Midlands.

"Before signing for Coventry I worked as a builder and played part-time football for Halesowen Town," says Sean.

"Part of my job on the building site was to carry bricks, often up and down ladders. That kind of thing, while keeping you generally fit, obviously helps to strengthen your legs.

"I wouldn't say that's the only reason I can jump so well, I think a lot of it is down to the fact that jumping high in the air just comes naturally to me and to the fact I get my timing right.

"I did the high-jump in athletics at school but wasn't an exceptional performer at the event, possibly because I was small. I'm not exactly big now, but I've been able to get up so well since before my non-league days.

"I'm now playing in the Premier League with Coventry City and jumping is still one of my fortes. I'm the first to admit that I'm not the most skilful player in the Premiership, my strengths are in my leaping and work-rate.

"But big defenders always look down and think that beating me to the high balls will be easy. They often have a shock when I reach the ball instead of them, but one of the reasons I am in the City side is to get up and knock the ball on.

"It has been put to me by people that as time goes on and other teams wise up to my talents I will become less effective, because teams will know all about what I can do and stop it.

"I don't agree with this point of view. Yes, they might get to know about me, but they won't be able to stop me unless they find someone in

their side who can jump higher than me.

"I don't practice my jumping, but since I started to play centre-forward at Coventry I have worked on my headers. When you play up front, you need a better touch and better finishing skills than as a midfielder."

The Premier League is a long way removed from Halesowen Town, and after watching a number of his team-mates move away from part-time football and into the big time, Sean can be forgiven for having wondered if he would ever make it at all.

"I was aware that professional clubs were watching me play non-league, but it always seemed to be a team-mate who was signed up," he continues.

"Andy Pearce, now with Sheffield Wednesday, Dean Spink who went to Aston Villa and Stuart Cash who joined Nottingham Forest all went before me.

"And even when Coventry did declare their interest, they only took me on a three-month trial.

"My father-in-law was my boss back then, so he gave me three months off work to try my hand as a footballer.

"I knew that I could go back and work for him if I didn't make it which took some pressure off me, but all I was really bothered about was becoming a full-time player.

"That obviously happened and after a spell working hard in the reserves, I finally made the first-team.

"People have asked me whether it took me time to get used to the rigours of full-time training. Actually, I thought non-league training was harder.

"After all, with Halesowen you would turn up for training after doing a full day's work. For me, that meant working on the building site all day Tuesday and Thursday before reporting for training, training which usually meant running."

Sean first established himself in Coventry's first-team as a wide mid-

field player, thrown in to flick the ball on for Coventry's speedy front men, Peter Ndlovu and John Williams.

But towards the end of last season, the 26-year-old forged out a centre-forward role for himself as Phil Neal's men found goals hard to come by.

"The team ended last season well by beating Blackburn and drawing away at Manchester United, but I was also pleased with my personal form late on," Sean continues.

"I played up front in the last seven or eight games and thoroughly enjoyed the experience. I had something of a free rein up there, could run around and harass defenders.

"The manager asked me if I wanted to go up front because we were a little short of goals. I have never been a natural goalscorer, but found the net a few times while playing in the position for the reserves.

"I was happy to move from the wing into the middle, though, and scored a couple of goals. I missed a few chances as well, but that's always likely to happen when a player is new to a position.

"I'm just glad to be a professional footballer, especially after combining part-time football with my work as a builder for so long."

Turn the page to see some other players with springs in their heels...⇨

jum...

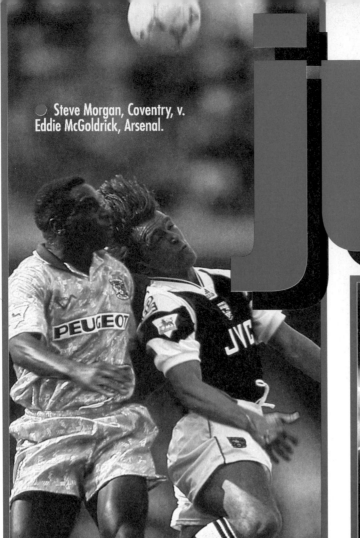

● Steve Morgan, Coventry, v. Eddie McGoldrick, Arsenal.

● David Kelly, Wolves, v. Mick Forsyth, Derby.

● Mark Hateley, Rangers, v. Willie Jamieson, Partick Thistle.

● Scott Leitch, Hearts, v. Peter Grant, Celtic.

p to it!

Colin Hendry, Blackburn, v. Guy Whittingham, Aston Villa.

Steve McManaman, Liverpool, v. Gary Kelly, Leeds.

FOOT-BALL'S VERSION OF AN AERIAL DOG-FIGHT!

Craig Short, Derby, v. Ian Ormondroyd, Leicester.

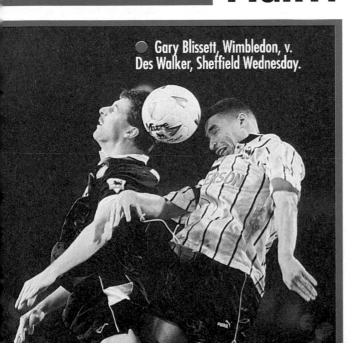

Rob Newman, Norwich, v. David Wetherall, Leeds.

Gary Blissett, Wimbledon, v. Des Walker, Sheffield Wednesday.

123

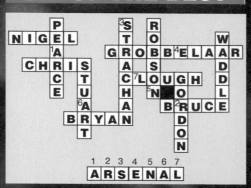

SIX OF THE BEST

Crossword solution with: NIGEL, PEARCE, CHRIS, STUART, STRACHAN, ROBSON, GROBBELAAR, WADDLE, LOUGH, GORDON, BRUCE, BRYAN

1 2 3 4 5 6 7
ARSENAL

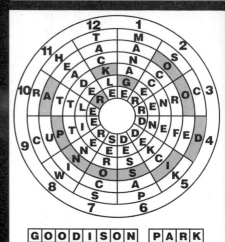

REVOLVER

GOODISON PARK

OH, NO! I GOT THEM ALL WRONG!

How well did **YOU** get on with the puzzles on pages 38 & 39? Here are the correct solutions...

SCRAMBLER

1 FULHAM
2 ARSENAL
3 LEEDS
4 CHELSEA
5 STOKE
6 RAITH
7 IPSWICH
8 PARTICK

CHARLTON

FLY THE FLAG

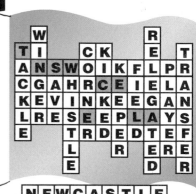

KEVIN KEEGAN

NEWCASTLE

STAR FILLING

BILL
ALAN
BRIAN
JOHN
DES
SID

your picture guide

ACTION!
COLOUR!
PIN-UPS!

Printed and Published in Great Britain by D. C. THOMSON & Co.,LTD185 Fleet Street, London EC4A 2HS.
© D. C. THOMSON & CO., LTD 1994
ISBN 0-85116-579-6

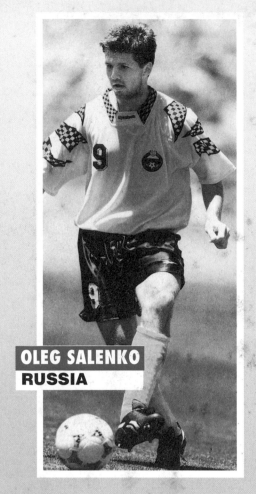

OLEG SALENKO
RUSSIA

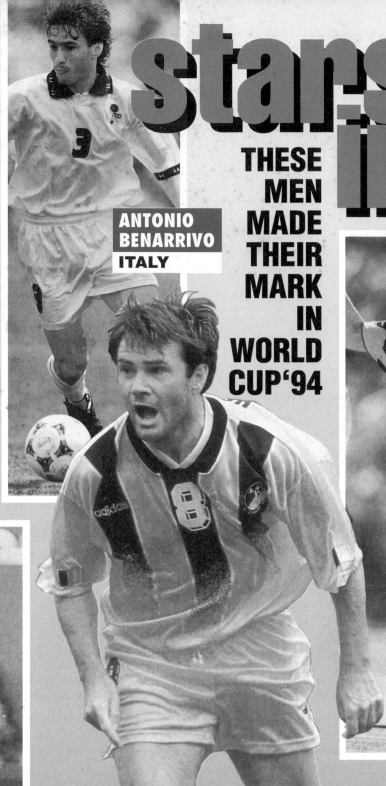

ANTONIO BENARRIVO
ITALY

stars in

THESE MEN MADE THEIR MARK IN WORLD CUP '94

BEBETO
BRAZIL

RAY HOUGHTON
REPUBLIC OF IRELAND